D1517589

A COZY BOOK OF WINTER DRINKS

RICH AND DELICIOUS RECIPES

TO KEEP YOU WARM

Susann Geiskopf-Hadler

PRIMA PUBLISHING

Published by Prima Publishing, Roseville, California. Member of the Crown Publishing Group, a division of Random House, Inc., New York.

PRIMA PUBLISHING and colophon are trademarks of Random House, Inc., registered with the United States Patent and Trademark Office.

Portions of this text were originally published in *A Cozy Book of Coffees & Cocoas* by Susann Geiskopf-Hadler, Prima Publishing, 1996.

Illustrations by Richard Sheppard.

Library of Congress Cataloging-in-Publication Data
Geiskopf-Hadler, Susann
   A cozy book of winter drinks : rich and delicious recipes to keep you warm / Susann Geiskopf-Hadler.
     p. cm.
   ISBN 0-7615-6368-7
   1. Beverages. I. Title. II. Series.

TX815.G45   2002
641.8'7—dc21   2002070521

02 03 04 05 AA 10 9 8 7 6 5 4 3 2 1
Printed in the United States of America

First Edition

Visit us online at www.primapublishing.com

Contents

Recipe List

Recipes for Cozy Coffee and Cocoa Drinks

Introduction

Have you ever wondered about the origin of coffee, where chocolate comes from, or how brandy and other spirits came to be? *A Cozy Book of Winter Drinks* not only presents tasty recipes, but also explores the legendary history surrounding the discovery of coffee. Investigate the origin of collecting and transforming cocoa beans from the *Theobroma cacao* plant—"food of the Gods"—into chocolate. Revisit the earliest experiments by monks and healers who mixed herbs with fermenting fruit to produce cures for the common ailments of the day. Learn how the method of distillation was discovered, thus giving birth to many of today's popular spirits.

We drink a lot of liquid each day to quench our thirst, so the recipes in this book are intended to please our palates! Read them for inspiration and then create what you like. Exact measurements are given for all of the cozy and spirited drinks presented, and I suggest that you follow the recipes at first and then, as with cooking, experiment to develop your own personal favorites.

The duty of being a home bartender or of making coffee house–style beverages can be intimidating. We'll explore techniques for shaken, stirred, and blended drinks, as well as coffee brewing methods. You'll also find helpful preparation tips. Master the simple techniques presented in this book, and you will get the reputation among family and friends for making "the best" cappuccino, martini, or special hot cocoa. Presentation is also important, so choosing the perfect mug, stemware, or glass is essential. A special section is included to guide you in selecting and stocking your shelves with an eclectic mix of the perfect serving vessels.

The recipes in *A Cozy Book of Winter Drinks*—whether alcohol based, espresso drinks, or hot cocoa—are so delicious that you will savor each one and look forward to the next occasion to gather with family or friends and enjoy your favorite cozy beverages.

1

INGREDIENTS FOR SPIRITED DRINKS

At the heart of each spirited drink is a key ingredient. Many of these ingredients, such as gin, vodka, brandy, or whiskey, come from the centuries-old process known as distillation. Heat is used to separate the components of a liquid, or mash, and as vaporization takes place, the liquid is cooled and condensed into a neutral spirit with little color, aroma, or flavor. The distiller uses the art of blending to add flavors and the right degree of aging to achieve the desired spirit before bottling.

Traditionally, liqueurs were made by either infusion (steeping flavoring agents in water) or maceration (steeping flavoring agents in alcohol). When the still was invented in the Middle Ages, flavoring agents and alcohol were distilled together in a still pot. Today, spirits may also be percolated or dripped through flavoring agents until optimum flavor is achieved. All liqueurs must contain at least 2.5 percent sugar by weight, although the amount varies depending on the formula used by the individual distiller. Liqueurs are made from formulas that are trade secrets, closely guarded and passed from one generation to the next.

History and Folklore

Pure water was not always the commonplace beverage that it is today. During the Middle Ages, pure water was unknown in the cities, and waterborne diseases were rampant. To avoid stomach disorders, one had to avoid water. In those days, it was common to enjoy a pint of ale at breakfast and other spirits, coffee, or tea throughout the day. Each region within a country developed its unique signature distillations based on ingredients common to the area. Thus were born key regional beverages that are still popular today.

Many spirited distillations also had medicinal properties. Gin was first discovered in an attempt to develop a cure for tropical diseases that sailors on Dutch East India Company ships brought back to the Netherlands in the seventeenth century. Dr. Sylvius, a professor of medicine at the University of Leiden, did not discover a cure, but he did discover something that acted as a mild sedative when taken in moderation. This infusion of juniper berries was touted to be a mild diuretic and a vasodilator, beneficial for many types of cardiac conditions, as well as a stimulant to the appetite and a tonic for the elderly. Dr. Sylvius called his tonic *aqua vitae,* "vital water," although his countrymen called it *jenever.* The French variation was *genièvre,* which translated to "gin" once the drink became common in England. The English distillers increased the amount of corn malt relative to barley malt, so their gin developed its own pronounced flavor, which tended to be lighter in body and taste, with a clean juniper flavor. *Jenever*

still retains its original full-bodied flavor and malty aroma, and the gin widely available in today's market reflects the English style of distillation.

Brandy was associated with its own properties during the Middle Ages. Arnaud de Villeneuve, from the Charente region of France, wrote of the medicinal properties of a local spirit known to alleviate sickness and prolong life. The capital of the region is none other than Cognac, which now shares its name with the "royal family" of the brandy world.

In search of medicines, doctors and monks produced the first liqueurs hundreds of years ago by mixing honey or sugar with bitter herb elixirs for their patients. Benedictine is a noted example. This amber-colored herbal liqueur was named after the Benedictine monks who first produced it in 1510.

Today, many distilled beverages are available around the world. Those commonly used in our cozy recipes are discussed below.

Brandy is often referred to as eau-de-vie, "the water of life."

Distillations from Grapes

Even though grapes are a fruit, distillations from grapes make up their own category. We commonly think of wine and champagne when we think of grapes, but the distillation process is also used to produce brandy and cognac.

Brandy

Brandy was probably first produced as a result of the invention of the still during the middle of the thirteenth century in France. Then known as *eau-de-vie*, "water of life," it is now produced around the world wherever grapes are grown. After two distillations, the clear, colorless alcohol is place in wooden barrels to age. The barrels are usually made of oak and give the brandy its distinctive nutty brown color and unique flavor. Brandy is also produced from other fruits; those products will be discussed below.

A cordial—another term for liqueur—is often served as an after-dinner drink.

Cognac

Cognac, perhaps the best-known brandy in the world, comes from an area in western France around the town of Cognac. This brandy can only be made from specific white grapes that are grown and distilled within the strictly defined geographical area of the Charente region. Cognac production is closely governed by old traditions and by French laws.

Wines

Red and white wines are produced in many countries around the world. Microclimates and soil mineral content produce unique distinctive qualities within the same grape varieties. The grapes are crushed and then fermented in barrels or in stainless-steel tanks, after which the juice is transferred to oak barrels for further aging. The winemaker's signature touch will shape the final product. Wine has been enjoyed for centuries as a stand-alone drink and as an ingredient in drink recipes.

Champagne

Champagne is made predominantly from the chardonnay and pinot noir grapes. To be called "champagne" in France, it must be made in the Champagne region of France and fermented in the bottle in which it is sold—*methode champenoise*. Other areas of the world produce excellent sparkling wines, but they usually bear different names, such as cave, crémant, or spumante. Vintage champagne or sparkling wine is produced from grapes of a particular year, whereas nonvintage is a blend—cuvée—of wine from a variety of years, which is used to produce a finished product that conforms to the particular winemaker's style. Most champagne ferments in the bottle—*méthode champenoise*—as it goes through a laborious riddling process. Bottles are stored at a slight angle and then turned several degrees at stipulated times to agitate the yeast and sugars to enhance the fermentation process.

Distillations from Fruits

Frequently, more fruit ripens at one time than can be consumed. Many varieties of fruit brandy were developed to utilize the excess. Practically any fruit can be used, although some require the addition of sugar or alcohol since their natural fruit sugar content is too low for fermentation to take place.

Calvados

Calvados, a type of apple brandy, comes from the Normandy region in northwestern France, and under French law, the name "calvados" can be applied only to the distillation of this specific region's cider, famous for its crisp, clean apple flavor. After distillation, the apple cider is stored in oak or chestnut barrels and matured for at least two years, yielding an amber to light brown beverage. Calvados may be enjoyed before or after a meal. Sometimes a small amount is served in the middle of a meal to aid digestion and enhance one's appetite for the courses to come. Apple brandy produced in the United States is known as applejack.

Kirsch

Kirsch, a well-known liqueur from France, is made from fully ripe or fermenting cherries. Because its natural fruit sugar is so high, no additional sugar or alcohol is needed to enhance fermentation.

We all enjoy the sound of a cork popping out of a champagne bottle, but this allows precious bubbles to escape. Instead, wrap a towel around the neck of a chilled bottle, remove the foil and undo the wire, tip the bottle slightly, and slowly wiggle the cork out.

Framboise

Framboise is a popular fruit brandy with a mild, sweet taste. Because it is made from raspberries that are naturally low in sugar, alcohol is added before distillation to enhance the fermentation.

Cassis

Cassis is produced from black currants and gets its name from the French word for this berry. Cassis is also produced as crème de cassis, which has a lower alcohol content by volume and a lower sugar content than cassis. In France, cassis is usually served neat—straight up—as an aperitif. Crème de cassis frequently shows up as an ingredient in mixed drinks.

Distillations from Grains

Grains, including corn, not only are important food sources but have been utilized throughout the centuries to produce fine spirits. Gin, whiskey, and vodka are all part of this extended family of grain-based distilled spirits.

Gin

Gin is an alcohol distilled from barley and rye, to which a mixture of selected herbs and spices, known as botanicals, is added. The signature of a specific gin is determined by a secret blend of botanicals. The most common ingredients

The term "aperitif" refers to a drink that is enjoyed before a meal to "open up the appetite."

8

used are angelica root, aniseed, cardamom seeds, coriander, juniper berries, orris (iris) root, licorice, lemon peel, orange peel, almonds, cassia bark, caraway seeds, fennel, cinnamon bark, bergamot, and cocoa. The first distillation produces a neutral grain spirit, which is diluted with distilled water and then distilled once more in a "gin still" with the botanical flavoring agents of choice.

Vodka

Vodka is refined liquor that is traditionally processed to have no discernible taste, color, or odor. The unique characteristics of different brands of vodka stem from the types of grains used, the distillation methods, the filtration techniques, and the water used to control the alcohol strength. The Russians have contributed much to the art of distilling vodka. The technique of filtering vodka through charcoal, which gives vodka its clean taste, was developed in 1810 by a pharmaceutical chemist named Audry Albanov and is used by most distillers today. It is unclear if vodka was invented by the Russians or the Poles, as historical documentation points to deep roots in both countries going as far back as the tenth century. Vodka, or "wodka," is the diminutive term for water, hailing from the Latin *aqua vitae* or "water of life." Specific but subtle flavor characteristics also come from the minerals

in the water that is added to control the alcohol strength. Today, some brands of vodka, especially those from Scandinavian countries, are flavored with caraway seeds, dill seeds, lemon, lime, or pepper. These flavored vodkas are becoming very popular in the United States and are the key ingredient in specific mixed drinks.

Whiskey

Whiskey, as spelled by the Americans and the Irish, or whisky, as the Canadians and Scots spell it, is the most widely drunk liquor in the world. Scottish whisky, or Scotch, is produced from malted barley or a mixture of grains that can include corn or wheat. It is aged for at least three years in oak casks—usually casks that previously aged sherry—before being bottled. Scotch can be blended or single malt. Blended Scotch contains malt and grain whiskies from several distilleries blended together. If the label states an age, it will represent how long the "youngest" whiskey in the blend was aged in the cask. Single malts are produced strictly from malted barley and frequently have a distinctive smoky aroma that comes from drying the barley malt grains over burning peat from the Scottish moorlands.

Irish whiskey is made from barley, wheat, rye, or oats. After distillation, clear water is added to bring the whiskey to its final alcoholic content of about 80 proof. Irish whiskey is matured in wooden casks for at least three years. These casks will have previously stored rum, sherry, or bourbon, which impart unique flavors to the finished whiskey. Irish whiskey tends to be mellower than Scotch.

To further complicate this category, the American corn-based liquor is known as bourbon. The key ingredient is corn mash, but small amounts of rye and barley malt are also used. After distillation, bourbon is matured for at least two years—but frequently six years or longer—in new white-oak casks that have had the insides charred. This adds the unique coloration to the whiskey and lends a slightly sweet vanilla flavor. Bourbon can be produced straight (meaning that it is distilled from a single grain and bottled by a single distiller) or blended.

Bourbon, rye whiskey, and corn whiskey are blended to produce American blended whiskey. Canadian whisky is blended from straight grain whiskies, yielding a somewhat flavorless alcohol that is an excellent choice for mixed drinks.

Distillations from Plants and Roots

It seems that almost anything can be used in the production of spirits. Some popular distillations in this category are

A highball is served in a highball or collins glass with a few ice cubes. This preparation is usually a shot of liquor combined with a soft-drink mixer, resulting in a perfect thirst-quencher.

derived from by-products, such as molasses from sugar production. Others come from thorny plants.

Ouzo

Ouzo is a popular anise-flavored Greek liqueur. It is slightly sweet and has a very high alcohol content.

Rum

Rum is made from a by-product of sugarcane refining. This brown, viscous molasses is its central ingredient. After distillation, rum is clear and colorless. Light rum is placed in pale ash-wood barrels for only one year and then transferred into stainless-steel tanks for further aging. It has a delicate taste and is well suited for use as an ingredient in cocktails. Dark rum is left to mature for five to seven years in darker wooden casks, where it develops its golden color and full-flavored body. The Caribbean Islands are the home of rum, with distillers on each island—as well as distillers along the Atlantic Coast of the United States, Central America, and South America—all offering a distinctive signature flavor in their rum.

Tequila

Tequila's roots date back to the time of the Aztec civilization. The first extracts from this plant were called *aguamiel*, Spanish

Centuries ago, distilled spirits were quite harsh so they were frequently infused with herbs, fruits, or flower blossoms.

for "holy water." Tequila, Mexico's number one spirit, is distilled from the juice of one variety of the manguey plant, *Agave tequilana weber*, or blue agave. Most tequila is produced in a specific geographical region around the town of Tequila; hence the name. Tequileros cultivate the blue agave, which grows for ten years before it is ready for harvest. At that time the "heart" of the agave is harvested and then roasted in a huge steam oven. The juice is then pressed out, and sugar is added; the mix ferments for four days. This distillation is repeated until the desired alcohol content is reached. The resulting clear, white tequila—sometimes called "silver" tequila— is bottled immediately after distillation and is ready to drink. Tequila anejo—gold tequila—is stored for several years in oak barrels. The flavor mellows during this time, becoming smooth, and the color turns to a light golden brown. It is common to enjoy well-aged tequila neat—straight up with salt and lime—but tequila also marries well as an ingredient in cocktails.

Liqueurs

Hundreds of years ago, doctors and monks unknowingly produced the first liqueurs in their search for medicines. Their mixtures of bitter herbal elixirs were sweetened with honey or sugar to make them palatable. Today, liqueurs are distillates of plants, fruit juices, or essential oils and are often sweetened with honey or sugar. Liqueurs can also have cream, coffee, chocolate, or eggs as their base ingredient.

Amaretto

Amaretto is produced in Italy from sweet and bitter almonds, apricot kernels, vanilla, and a mix of spices. The resulting amber-colored liqueur is free of the prussic acid that is contained in almonds and apricot pits, as it is separated out during distillation.

Anisette

Anisette is a bitter liqueur from France. The primary ingredient is star anise, which is blended with ingredients such as fennel, cloves, coriander, orris root, and other spices. Anisette is frequently used in cooking.

Cointreau

Cointreau is a cognac-based liqueur that is flavored with ripe Seville or Curaçao oranges. It is usually drunk neat—straight up—or over ice but is also used as an ingredient in cocktails and baked goods.

Coffee Liqueurs

Coffee liqueurs, also called mocha, are produced from freshly roasted and ground coffee beans or from powdered coffee. The base alcohol is usually vodka. Kahlúa is a popular Mexican coffee-based liqueur flavored with herbs and vanilla beans, and Tia Maria is a favorite that comes from Jamaica, using rum as its base.

Crèmes

This category of liqueur has many stars. Most of them have cognac or brandy as their base, and they usually get their characteristic flavor from fruit distillates. Contrary to what their names suggest, they are usually not dairy based. Crème de cassis comes from black currants, crème de coco from coconuts, and crème de framboise from raspberries. Crème de menthe is available in a green or white preparation and smells and tastes like peppermint. Crème de cacao is a liqueur made from roasted and shelled cocoa beans with a touch of vanilla. Crème de café is a coffee liqueur made from freshly roasted and ground coffee beans.

Drambuie

Drambuie is a signature liqueur from Scotland. The base is 15-year-old Scotch that is mixed with highland herbs and heather-flower honey.

Frangelico

Frangelico, the Italian herb liqueur, is made from hazelnuts, herbs, and berries.

Galliano

Galliano is a very notable Italian liqueur. The unique flavor of this traditionally golden yellow liqueur comes from a blend of more than 70 different herbs and plant extracts.

Grand Marnier

Grand Marnier is the quintessential blend of Caribbean bitter oranges and French cognac. It is usually served in a brandy snifter or chilled over ice in a rocks glass. The unique flavor also adds interest to cozy mixed drinks.

Sambuca

Sambuca is an Italian liqueur that gets its licorice flavor from aniseed. Other licorice-flavored liqueurs are available, but only Sambuca has elderberries, which contribute to its unique flavor.

Fortified Wines

A fortified wine has a blend of sugar or honey added to it. This not only yields interesting characteristics but also ex-

tends shelf life. Some common fortified wines are port, sherry, and vermouth.

Port Wine

Port wine, or Vinho do Porto, originates in a strictly controlled area of Portugal known as the Douro region. Red and ruby ports are young blends with a slightly sweet and fruity taste. Enjoy port as a dessert wine or as an ingredient in an elegant cocktail.

Sherry

Sherry is a fortified wine from the Mediterranean that is produced in the area around Jerez in the south of Spain known as the "Sherry Triangle." Different types of sherry are distinguished according to taste. Fino is the driest sherry and is straw yellow in color with a slight scent of almonds. Manzanilla is a specific fino from Sanlucar de Barrameda that is light and fresh with a slightly bitter, dry flavor. Amontillado is amber colored and available in a medium or medium-dry finish. Oloroso is a dark brown sherry that tastes faintly of walnuts. Cream sherry is probably the most common. It is an oloroso that has been sweetened by adding wine made from Pedro Ximinez—muscatel grapes. It is sweet and dark.

> Claret is the liquor for boys;
> Port for men;
> But he who aspires to be a
> hero must drink brandy.
> —Dr. Samuel Johnson

Vermouth

Vermouth is produced mostly in France and Italy. It is wine fortified with herbs, alcohol, sugar, and caramel. Dry vermouth is always white, whereas semisweet vermouth is also available as a rosé.

Bitters

Bitters are aromatic mixtures of various botanicals in an alcoholic base. Ingredients such as seeds, roots, leaves, bark, fruits, and stems—mostly tropical or subtropical in origin— are used to produce signature bitters from coveted recipes. The term "bitters" encompasses both liqueurs served as aperitifs and those used as an ingredient in mixed drinks.

Angostura Bitters

Angostura Aromatic Bitters is a well-known brand of bitters and is readily available. A surgeon, Dr. Johann Gottlieb Benjamin Siegert, first formulated it in 1824. Seville orange peel, angelica, cardamom, cinnamon, and cloves are some of the ingredients in this closely guarded recipe. This bitter is used in small quantities to give a drink, such as an old-fashioned, its distinctive flavor.

Campari

Campari is a common bitter aperitif consumed in Italy with a splash of soda or tonic water. Some mixed drinks call for a splash of Campari as a flavor accent. Campari was created in Milan in 1861 by a distiller named Divide Campari, from a mixture of herbs and Seville orange peel.

Specialty Ingredients

Personal taste comes into play when choosing what beverages, spices, and coffees should stock your bar. Begin with some basic ingredients and build on them as you discover your own signature style. Price does not always dictate what is best. Purchase what you can afford, or what tastes best to you.

✦ *Distillations from grapes:* brandy, cognac, red wine, white wine, and champagne are the most frequently used.

✦ *Distillations from fruit:* kirsch, framboise, cassis, and other fruit brandies are nice varieties to have on hand.

✦ *Distillations from grain:* gin, whiskey, and vodka are commonly used.

✦ *Distillations from plants and roots:* rum and tequila come into play in some drinks.

19

- ❖ *Liqueurs:* amaretto, anisette, crèmes, Drambuie, Frangelico, and Grand Marnier all have their place in a well-stocked bar.

- ❖ *Fortified wines:* port, sherry, and vermouth are frequently used.

- ❖ *Spices:* nutmeg, cinnamon sticks, and whole cloves are used in many hot, cozy drinks.

- ❖ *Garnishes:* lemons, limes, oranges, pineapple, mint leaves, cherries, olives, and cocktail onions should all be kept on hand. Use only unwaxed, organic citrus fruits for garnishes and for squeezing into drinks or for adding to punches.

Homemade Kahlúa is easy to make. Mix 2 ounces powdered espresso and 4 cups sugar into 2 cups boiling water. Whisk to dissolve and set aside to cool. Add 2 cups vodka and stir to thoroughly blend. Transfer into a jar or bottle that has a tight-fitting lid. Slice 2 whole vanilla beans lengthwise and place them in the bottle. Secure the lid and store for about a month in a cool, dark place. Decant into smaller bottles, removing the vanilla bean.

2

TOOLS AND TECHNIQUES FOR SPIRITED DRINKS

Preparing a cozy drink can be as enjoyable as consuming it. Make sure that you stock your home bar with some basic tools that will enable you to easily prepare specialty drinks. Some everyday kitchen gadgets can be put into use; however, you will need to buy a few things. When you shop for specific bar equipment, purchase items that are easy to clean. Stainless-steel and glass utensils are my first choice. These tools will, with a little practice, make preparation fun and may entice your guests to join in the process.

Basic Equipment for the Cozy Bar

There are many gadgets in specialty stores designated for the home bar. The ones described below are essential for easy preparation of spirited and cozy drinks.

Cocktail Shaker
An essential tool used for making the classic martini, the cocktail shaker will also come in handy for mixing the ingredients for many other drinks. I like the standard stainless-steel, three-part shaker, which consists of a beaker, a lid, and a built-in strainer. The lid fits tightly, allowing you to really shake up spirits, juices, or cream-based concoctions. The strainer will hold back pieces of ice, fruit pits, or seeds when you pour the cocktail.

Bar Sieve

A round, stainless-steel strainer (also called a bar strainer), a bar sieve is used when drinks are mixed in a mixing glass. The edge of a bar strainer is rimmed with a coiled spring, and the center has holes allowing only the liquid to pass through as the drink is poured into a serving glass, leaving behind the ice or pieces of fruit.

Bar Spoon

This long-handled spoon is a versatile tool that comes in handy for stirring ingredients in a mixing glass. It can also be used for measuring: the spoon holds 1/6 ounce of liquid, the same amount as a standard kitchen teaspoon. The rounded back of the spoon is used to slowly pour layers of liquors into a glass when you want the layers to float on, rather than mix into, the drink. At the top of the 10-inch handle is usually a disc called a muddler. This is used to crush, or muddle, pieces of fruit, herbs, or sugar cubes.

Bar Measure

Also called a pony-jigger measure, this double-ended measure allows you to determine exact quantities. The pony cup is a 1-ounce measure, and the jigger is a 1 1/2- to 2-ounce measure. Purchase one that is made of stainless steel with easy-to-read 1/4-ounce and 1/2-ounce markings inside the jigger end.

Ice can easily become contaminated by freezer odors. It is best to use a fresh bag of ice for mixed drinks. If the ice-maker in your freezer is a separate compartment from the rest of your freezer, the ice should be odor free.

25

Standard kitchen measuring spoons can also be used—3 teaspoons (1 tablespoon) is equal to $1/2$ ounce, $41/2$ teaspoons is equal to $3/4$ ounce, and 2 tablespoons is equal to 1 ounce.

Citrus Juicer

A stainless-steel or glass manual citrus juicer is recommended for extracting fresh lemon, lime, and orange juice. A standard model will have a place for manually twisting and reaming the fruit, or you can get the model that entails placing the fruit on an extraction disc and pulling a top piece down over the fruit.

Mixing Glass

Sometimes referred to as a shaker glass, this vessel is used for drinks that are stirred, not shaken. Purchase one with a capacity of about 1 quart, which will allow you to make three to four drinks at one time.

The Art of Essential Glassware

Suitable stemware and mugs will make your drinks dazzle. Imaginative cozy drinks call for the appropriate glass or mug to properly show them off. Build your collection as you go, starting with the glasses or mugs that accommodate the

A "shot" refers to a measure of alcohol or espresso ranging from 1 to 2 ounces.

drinks you most frequently prepare. And they don't all have to match. An eclectic set will allow each guest to identify his or her drink. Shop at yard sales and secondhand, specialty, and department stores for a wonderful variety of styles and shapes. Keep seasonal and event-oriented coasters, napkins, and candles on hand to set the mood of the gathering.

Brandy Snifter

A snifter has a short stem and a balloon-shaped bowl. Warm or room-temperature drinks should be served in this type of glass. Snifters range in size from 3 to 12 ounces.

Champagne Flute

The upright champagne flute, with its narrow opening, will show off not only champagne but also cream- and fruit-based drinks. This glass is quite elegant and typically holds from 4 to 7 ounces.

Champagne Saucer

This bowl-shaped glass on a stem allows bubbles to readily escape and typically holds about 4 ounces.

Cocktail Glass

Time-honored, this glass has sloping sides and a stem, making it the ideal glass for drinks served without ice—such as a

If you stack glasses and they stick together, remember this simple tip: Put the bottom glass in very warm water and fill the top glass with cold water. The bottom glass will expand slightly and the top glass will contract, allowing them to be separated easily.

martini. This Y-shaped glass ranges in size from 3 to 6 ounces. The solid, sturdy stem is designed to hold onto, so you don't warm the drink.

Collins Glass

Taller than a rocks glass, but with a sturdy bottom, this glass will accommodate many shaken or blended drinks. Collect clear or frosted ones ranging from 10 to 14 ounces in size.

Cordial Glass

Also known as a sherry glass, this glass is used to serve cordials, liqueurs, or mixed drinks. Fancy or plain, this glass will accommodate 3 to 4 ounces.

Hot Drink Mug

This mug always has a handle and is made to accommodate a hot drink. Many shapes and sizes are available, ranging from 10 to 12 ounces.

Paris Goblet

This balloon-shaped goblet is suitable for serving white or red wine, as well as beer, aperitifs, and various cocktails. Glass size ranges from 9 to 14 ounces.

A shot that is served "up" is shaken in a cocktail shaker with ice and served in a classic cocktail glass.

Rocks Glass

This short glass with a thick bottom is also known as a low-ball glass or an old-fashioned glass—the latter name made famous by the eponymous drink. It is the perfect size glass for a cocktail served on-the-rocks or with a splash of soda or water. Glass size ranges from 8 to 10 ounces.

Sherry Glass

A small, tulip-shaped glass that is used for liqueur and for serving fortified wines, aperitifs, and other short drinks. The typical sherry glass holds about 3 ounces.

Punch Glass

This squat glass has a wide opening and a handle, but not a stem. Use it for serving a hot or cold punch or mulled wine. A punch glass holds 4 to 6 ounces.

Shot Glass

A shot glass can be used to measure liquor, usually 1 1/2 ounces, or it can be used as a "shooter" to serve a shot of alcohol straight up. A "nervous" glass can also be used to serve a shot of liquor. It will accommodate almost 3 ounces but is commonly used to serve a standard shot.

Preheat a glass or mug by placing it in a 250 degree F oven for about 15 minutes. Remove from the oven with an oven mitt and set aside to cool slightly. You may also instantly heat a mug by filling it with hot water. Empty the hot water, drain briefly on a bar towel, then fill with your cozy drink, and serve immediately.

Wine Glass

A white wine glass has a tall stem and is tulip shaped. A classic red wine glass has a shorter stem and is also slightly tulip shaped. These glasses typically hold 10 to 14 ounces.

Basic Techniques for Preparing Spirited Drinks

When making the cozy drinks in this book, make sure you measure correctly, use the best ingredients that you can afford, and follow the directions. Serve warm drinks in warmed glasses or mugs, and cold drinks in chilled glasses. Use a fresh glass for each refill—this may seem extravagant, but it will ensure the best-tasting drink every time.

Cold drinks should always be made with fresh ice. Use ice made from filtered water that has been stored in a bag or an isolated area of the freezer where it will not be contaminated by freezer odors. Water used in hot drinks should also be filtered and free of any odors.

As with many things in life, the eye is the first to be aroused, so presentation of a drink is important. Choose the proper glass and then finish off the drink with the perfect garnish. Some drinks command a classic garnish, such as an olive in a martini, a cherry in a manhattan, or whipped cream

"Neat" is a classic term used to describe serving liquor—usually whiskey—straight up in a shot glass. Liquor served this way is not chilled.

sprinkled with cocoa on hot chocolate. Others allow you to be creative. Just remember to use ingredients that are suitable for the drink in both taste and color.

How to Shake a Drink

The cocktail shaker blends ingredients by vigorous shaking. Place ice in the cocktail shaker, filling it about two-thirds full. Add the ingredients and tightly close the shaker. Shake for 10 to 20 seconds so the ingredients are chilled and slightly aerated in the shaker. Serve the drink, usually in a cocktail glass, by pouring it through the built-in strainer, leaving the ice and any fruit in the shaker.

How to Stir a Drink

Drink recipes that require less blending are stirred. A shaker quickly chills the ingredients but also adds small air bubbles that can cloud a clear liquid; hence the debate over the stirred, not shaken, martini. Be careful to avoid overstirring drinks made with champagne or sodas; you don't want to spoil the fizz.

To prepare a drink in the glass it will be served in, place ice cubes in a chilled glass. Add the ingredients according to the recipe, and then carefully stir the drink using a bar spoon. Garnish, if desired, and serve immediately.

Prechill a glass by placing it in the refrigerator for about an hour. An instant method is to fill a glass with ice water, set it aside, and prepare the drink. Dump out the ice water, drain briefly on a bar towel, then fill the glass with the prepared drink, and serve immediately.

31

Sometimes a drink will be mixed in a mixing glass and then strained through a bar sieve into the serving glass. Garnish and serve immediately.

How to Float Liqueur

Some hot drink recipes call for a "float" of liqueur. This is very simple to create. Put all the ingredients except the alcohol in a glass. Hold a bar spoon face down over the glass and slowly pour the liqueur over the back of the spoon. It will float on the top.

How to Garnish a Drink

A garnish is used to decorate a drink. When using fresh fruit, make sure that it has been washed and is blemish free. Take care to slice it carefully—try using a potato peeler or citrus zester to cut the perfect twist for a drink.

How to Prepare a Hot Drink

Have all of your ingredients on hand. Preheat your serving glass or mug: fill it with hot water, discard the water, and place it upside down on a tea towel. Allow it to sit for a minute to dry, and then add all of the drink ingredients and serve.

To salt or sugar the rim of a glass, moisten the rim of the chilled glass with a lemon or lime wedge. Dip the rim into a saucer of salt or sugar.

Tips and Tricks of the Trade

As with any skill that you acquire, there are always the hidden
secrets that will produce the premium results. The same is
true in preparing cozy beverages.

✦ Follow the recipe exactly, measuring carefully.

✦ Cleanliness is paramount! Wash everything immediately
   after you use it, before you use it again to prepare the
   next drink. Use ice tongs or a fork and spoon to place ice
   cubes in the shaker glass.

✦ Chill glasses in the freezer for about 30 minutes if you
   want a "frost" on them, or place them in the refrigerator
   to make sure they are cold.

✦ Prepare any fancy garnishes in advance. When you serve a
   fruit-garnished drink, be sure to serve it with a small plate
   or cocktail napkin so that the drinker has a place to put
   the garnish when it is removed from the glass.

✦ Keep carbonated ingredients such as soft drinks, tonic
   water, mineral water, and champagne in the refrigerator.

✦ Do not use carbonated ingredients in a drink that is to be
   shaken—it will result in a mess as the contents fizz up and
   spill over the top.

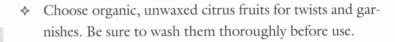

✦ Choose organic, unwaxed citrus fruits for twists and garnishes. Be sure to wash them thoroughly before use.

How to Taste a Drink

Quality, not quantity, comes into play here. Slow down and *enjoy* the drink. Allow your senses to come alive as you look at, smell, and taste it. Make sure your glasses are spotless and that the drink is neatly poured. As with food, the sense of smell is easily aroused. The mind remembers the subtle smells and flavors of toasted almonds or pecans, freshly sliced oranges or lemons, or ground cinnamon or nutmeg. Apply that knowledge when you create a drink. This is a pleasant experience, so indulge in it. Further engage your sense of smell by first sniffing your drink—especially a hot one—and then slowly sipping it. Consider the following criteria when enjoying a cozy drink.

✦ *Appearance.* Does the drink look appealing? The sense of sight gives a first impression, so take the time to add a garnish, such as a dash of freshly grated nutmeg.

✦ *Aroma.* Is there a signature smell that awakens you? Our sense of smell is stronger than our sense of taste, so allow it to introduce you to the drink.

- *Flavor.* Sip slowly, allowing the center, sides, and back of your tongue to experience the drink. We have many taste buds, primed to experience sweet, sour, salt, and spice flavors.

Measure for Measure

Traditionally, alcohol is measured by the ounce rather than by the teaspoon or tablespoon, so the recipes in this book are presented in this way. Drink recipes are designed to provide a single serving (except the punch recipes). Whatever you are making, use the indispensable bar measure to get predictable results every time. (See Basic Equipment for the Cozy Bar, page 24.) Sugar, honey, fruit juices, and other liquid ingredients are measured by the standard kitchen measuring spoons and measuring cups.

Small cheer and great welcome makes a merry feast.
—William Shakespeare

Measuring Guide
Reference this frequently so that you will have these equivalents memorized. They will come in handy every time you prepare drink recipes and will make you look like a pro!

1 tablespoon = $1/2$ ounce
$4 1/2$ teaspoons = $3/4$ ounce
2 tablespoons = 1 ounce

1 ounce = 1 pony
3 tablespoons = 1½ ounces
1½ ounces = 1 jigger

Equivalency Guide

How many times have you had to look up in a reference book how many ounces are in a half pint? This handy guide will serve as a quick reference tool.

8 fluid ounces = 1 cup = ½ pint
16 fluid ounces = 2 cups = 1 pint
1 quart = 4 cups = 2 pints
2 quarts = 8 cups = ½ gallon
4 quarts = 16 cups = 1 gallon
31½ gallons = 1 barrel

Approximate Measures

When shopping for ingredients, it is handy to know how many oranges or lemons you will need to yield a certain amount of juice. Some recipes call for an approximate but predictable measure such as a pinch. Follow these guidelines.

1 medium lemon = 3 tablespoons juice
1 medium lime = 2 tablespoons juice
1 medium orange = ⅓ cup juice

1 pinch = granules, usually of salt or pepper, that can be
   held between the thumb and forefinger
a dash = about 1/8 teaspoon
a splash = more than a dash, but less than a teaspoon

Traditional Bottle Sizes for Distilled Spirits

Alcohol traditionally was sold as a "pint" or a "fifth," and
that terminology is still with us, although bottle sizes now
carry metric measures. Refer to the old and new standards
when stocking your cozy bar. A standard serving per person is
about 1 1/2 ounces.

half pint = 8 oz. = 200 ml. = 6.8 oz. = 4 1/2 servings
pint = 16 oz. = 500 ml. = 16.9 oz. = 11 1/4 servings
fifth = 25.6 oz. = 750 ml. = 25.4 oz. = 17 servings
quart = 32 oz = 1 liter = 33.8 oz. = 22 servings
half gallon = 64 oz. = 1.76 liters = 59.2 oz. = 39 1/2 servings

Traditional Bottle Sizes for Still and Sparkling Wine

This reference will give you a good idea of how much wine to
purchase when having a dinner party. A standard serving is
about 4 1/4 ounces. This guide will also aid you in the purchase of still or sparkling wine to be used as an ingredient for
some of the punch recipes in this book.

Experiment with flavoring vodka (or gin), by adding fresh fruit or herbs to a liter of vodka and allowing it to infuse for 24 hours. Strain and store the vodka in the freezer. Anise seeds, ginger-root, and lemon peel all yield a lovely flavor accent.

37

split = 187 ml. = 6.3 oz. = 1 1/2 servings
tenth = 375 ml. = 12.7 oz. = 3 servings
fifth = 750 ml. = 25.4 oz. = 6 servings
quart = 1 liter = 1,000 ml. = 33.8 oz. = 8 servings
magnum = 1.5 liters = 50.7 oz. = 12 servings
double magnum = 3 liters = 101.4 oz. = 24 servings

3

RECIPES FOR COZY SPIRITED DRINKS

A cozy seasonal party, birthday gathering, or special event calls for a distinctive drink to set the mood. Planning the next vacation with friends might begin with a theme drink. A card game night will be even more fun with a hot, cozy drink in hand. Caroling during the holiday season calls for a warm-up drink. Also, seasonal parties demand easy-to-serve punches that are made ahead of time. I like to pair my beverages with a bit of food, so you will find serving suggestions sprinkled throughout this chapter.

Mastering the basic techniques discussed in chapter 2 will make you a skilled and confident bartender. Plan ahead so that you have all of your ingredients at hand, and have the glassware or mugs set out ready to chill or heat as needed.

Follow the recipes in this chapter, discover what you like, and then feel free to experiment. Drink recipes are presented in single servings, as they are quick to prepare and best mixed individually. The punch recipes give a specific number of servings and are designed to be prepared ahead of time. Enjoy!

Shaken and Stirred Cocktails

As a child growing up in England, I watched my parents hosting lavish cocktail parties. The women would be dressed

Wash your glasses immediately after each use, or soak them in warm soapy water. Once washed, place them rim down on a towel to dry overnight, or dry with one towel and polish with another.

in their fancy gowns with beautiful jewelry and the men in formal dinner jackets or military uniform. The food would be set out and the bar fully stocked. It was always cold there, so I am sure that these drinks made everyone feel cozy and warm. I used to peek down through the banister, thinking how grand it was! We don't dress that formal anymore for such gatherings, but the food and drinks can be just as elegant.

Gin Cassis Cocktail

This cocktail is a lovely shade of pink with a balance of slightly sweet and slightly sour flavors. The slice of lemon peel is the perfect color accent. Enjoy as a before-dinner aperitif, served with sliced pears, smoked cheese, and a fresh baguette.

YIELD: 1 SERVING

1 1/2 ounces gin
1/2 ounce crème de cassis
1/2 ounce freshly squeezed lemon juice
Twist of lemon peel

Fill a cocktail shaker about 2/3 full of crushed ice. Add the gin, crème de cassis, and lemon juice. Shake for about a minute, and then strain into a chilled cocktail glass. Garnish with the twist of lemon.

To get the full essence, twist the peel of a citrus fruit above the drink and then drop it into the glass.

Melting Martini

The fun name for this martini is to suggest not that it is frozen but that—if you are a martini fan—it will melt in your mouth. John Orr first served me his signature martini on New Year's Eve 1999, as we all held our collective breath in anticipation as to what the year 2000 would bring. Now that is history, but the drink lives on. This is a good before-dinner aperitif. Serve with crab spread, smoked oysters, and crackers.

YIELD: 1 SERVING

Several drops dry vermouth
1 1/2 ounces gin
2 olives

Place several drops of vermouth in a chilled cocktail glass. Swirl the vermouth around to coat the inside of the glass, and then pour out any residual. Fill a cocktail shaker about 2/3 full of crushed ice. Add the gin, and shake for about a minute. Strain into the vermouth-coated cocktail glass. Place the olives on a long toothpick, garnish the drink, and serve immediately.

Classic Gibson

Basically, this is the classic martini, but made with vodka and served with cocktail onions. Some bartenders suggest blotting the onions to remove any extra vinegar that might taint the flavor of the drink, but I

Get me out of this wet coat and into a dry martini.

—Robert Benchley

have friends who like to add some juice from the onion jar. Please your own palate.

YIELD: 1 SERVING

1 1/2 ounces vodka
1/2 teaspoon dry vermouth
2 pickled pearl onions

Fill a cocktail shaker about 2/3 full of crushed ice. Add the vodka and vermouth and shake for about a minute. Strain into a chilled cocktail glass. Place the onions on a long toothpick, garnish the drink, and serve immediately.

Sour Apple Martini

Flavored vodka has become quite the rage over the past few years. Several different brands are available, and well worth the price. The bartenders at Zinfandel Grille in Sacramento, CA, feature Van Gough Apple Vodka in their version of this cocktail. This drink also calls for pucker as an ingredient. You will find this sour apple cordial at a well-stocked liquor store.

YIELD: 1 SERVING

1 ounce apple vodka
1/2 ounce pucker
1/2 ounce cranberry juice
Thin slice of green apple

Fill a cocktail shaker about 2/3 full of crushed ice. Add the vodka, pucker, and cranberry juice and shake for about a

minute. Strain into a chilled cocktail glass. Garnish the drink with a thin slice of green apple, and serve immediately.

Lemon Drop

This cocktail uses flavored vodka. My friend Paul Bennett prefers Absolute Citron Vodka, but there are other lemon vodkas on the market.

YIELD: 1 SERVING

1 1/2 ounces citron vodka
1/2 ounce sweet and sour mix
1/2 ounce simple syrup (see sidebar)

Fill a cocktail shaker about 2/3 full of crushed ice. Add the vodka, sweet and sour mix, and simple syrup and shake for about a minute. Sugarcoat the rim of a chilled cocktail glass, then strain the drink into the glass. Serve immediately.

Cosmopolitan

Invite some friends over and catch up on life over a cosmopolitan or two. Serve a smoked salmon spread with baguette slices and Gouda cheese. You can use either Cointreau or Grand Marnier in this cocktail—they are both a bitter orange liqueur, but each has its own unique flavor.

YIELD: 1 SERVING

1 1/2 ounces vodka
1/2 ounce Cointreau or Grand Marnier

Simple syrup, also known as sugar syrup, is easy to make. Heat 1 1/2 cups water in a saucepan over medium heat and add 3/4 cup sugar. Continue to heat until the sugar dissolves. Increase the heat and boil for about 10 minutes. Pour into a jar and refrigerate until needed. Simple syrup can be purchased ready-made; Dan Good and Trader Vic's are good choices.

44

1 ounce cranberry juice
1/4 ounce lime juice
Sliver of orange peel

Fill a cocktail shaker about 2/3 full of crushed ice. Add the vodka, Cointreau, cranberry juice, and lime juice, and shake for about a minute. Strain into a chilled cocktail glass, and garnish with a sliver of orange peel. Serve immediately.

Manhattan

This is one of the classic drinks that I can remember my parents serving at cocktail parties in the 1950s. For the bourbon drinker, this is equivalent to the perfect martini. Angostura Bitters are my favorite brand.

YIELD: 1 SERVING

1 1/2 ounces bourbon
1/2 ounce sweet vermouth
Dash of bitters
1 maraschino cherry

Fill a cocktail shaker about 2/3 full of crushed ice. Add the bourbon, sweet vermouth, and bitters, and shake for about a minute. Strain into a chilled cocktail glass. Garnish the drink with a maraschino cherry, and serve immediately.

A dry martini is made with gin and served with an olive. A sweet martini is made with gin and served with a cherry. A perfect martini is made with gin and served with a twist of lemon. A Gibson is a martini made with vodka and served with an onion.

Rastini

This is a delicious combination of vodka and Chambourd, a raspberry liqueur from France. Zinfandel Grille in Sacramento, CA, makes a particularly good Rastini!

YIELD: 1 SERVING

1 1/2 ounces vodka
1/2 ounce Chambourd
Twist of lemon peel

Fill a cocktail shaker about 2/3 full of crushed ice. Add the vodka and Chambourd, and then shake for about a minute. Strain into a chilled cocktail glass. Garnish with the twist of lemon, and serve immediately.

Porto Rico

Port is frequently served as an after-dinner drink, but blended in this cocktail it is a refreshing aperitif. Serve mixed nuts to nibble on.

YIELD: 1 SERVING

1 1/2 ounces ruby port
3/4 ounce Scotch
2 teaspoons freshly squeezed lemon juice
Slice of lemon or orange

> I've taken more good from alcohol than alcohol has taken from me.
> —Winston Churchill

Fill a cocktail shaker about ⅔ full of crushed ice. Add the port, Scotch, and lemon juice. Shake for about a minute, and then strain into a chilled cocktail glass. Garnish the cocktail with a lemon or orange slice.

Gin and Cognac Cocktail

This cocktail blends the Brit's favorite—gin—with the Frog's favorite— cognac. The result is delicious. Serve this drink as you and your guests prepare a classic cheese fondue for dinner.

YIELD: 1 SERVING

1 ounce gin
½ ounce cognac
2 teaspoons apricot brandy
Lemon wedge

Fill a cocktail shaker about ⅔ full of crushed ice. Add the gin, cognac, and apricot brandy. Shake for about a minute, and then strain into a cocktail glass. Garnish with the lemon wedge.

Sunny Susann Cocktail

While writing this book, I was president of Soroptimist International of Sacramento. We had a fund-raiser at a local comedy club—Laughs Unlimited in Old Sacramento—and Mary Wray, a club member, came up with this drink. The bartenders featured the drink that evening.

YIELD: 1 SERVING

1 ounce gin
1/2 ounce apricot brandy
3/4 ounce freshly squeezed orange juice
Spritz of fresh lemon

Fill a cocktail shaker about 2/3 full of crushed ice. Add the gin, brandy, orange juice, and lemon juice. Shake for about a minute, and then strain into a cocktail glass.

Soroptini

Playful and fun, this cocktail was featured at a Soroptimist International of Sacramento fund-raising event. Soroptimist clubs are found worldwide, made up of women in management and professional positions who work through service projects to advance human rights and the status of women. The bartenders said this cocktail is a good before-dinner aperitif.

YIELD: 1 SERVING

1 ounce vodka
1 ounce blue curaçao
1/2 ounce pineapple juice
Twist of lemon

Fill a cocktail shaker about 2/3 full of crushed ice. Add the vodka, curaçao, and pineapple juice. Shake for about a minute, and then strain into a cocktail glass. Garnish with the twist of lemon.

Cassis Cognac Cocktail

Cassis is the juice from black currants frequently served with champagne as a Kir Royale. Here it is shaken with cognac for a delicious after-dinner drink. Serve with your favorite chocolates.

YIELD: 1 SERVING

1 ounce crème de cassis
1 ounce cognac
Twist of lemon

Fill a cocktail shaker about $2/3$ full of crushed ice. Add the crème de cassis and cognac. Shake for about a minute, and then strain into a cocktail glass. Garnish with the twist of lemon.

Bloody Mary

Legend has it that this drink originated as a simple mix of tomato juice, vodka, salt, and pepper sometime in the early 1920s. The seasoned version that we enjoy today has evolved over the years. You may use vodka or gin, depending on your preference. This is a great drink to serve on a weekend morning when you have friends over for brunch.

YIELD: 1 SERVING

2 ounces tomato juice
1 ounce vodka
2 teaspoons lemon juice
$1/4$ teaspoon Worcestershire sauce

In the early 1920s, Harry's New York Bar in Paris was a favorite hangout for such expatriates as Ernest Hemingway, F. Scott Fitzgerald, and Gertrude Stein. It is believed that the first tomato and vodka cocktail was made there.

Dash of hot pepper sauce
Pinch of salt
Pinch of black pepper
6-inch stalk celery

Partially fill a rocks glass with ice, and add the tomato juice, vodka, lemon juice, Worcestershire sauce, and hot pepper sauce. Mix together, and then sprinkle with the salt and pepper. Garnish with the stalk of celery, and serve immediately.

Classic Bourbon Old-Fashioned

This drink is so famous that the standard rocks glass is frequently referred to as an old-fashioned glass. Many versions of this drink are popular, but I favor this one, which my friend Paul Bennett prepares.

YIELD: 1 SERVING

1 cube sugar
Generous dash of angostura bitters
1 maraschino cherry, without stem
1/4 orange slice, with peel
1 1/2 ounces bourbon
Splash of soda
Slice of orange
1 maraschino cherry, with stem

Place the sugar, bitters, cherry without stem, and ¼ orange slice in the bottom of a rocks glass, and muddle them together with the end of your bar spoon. Add ice cubes to the glass, and pour in the bourbon and desired amount of soda. Garnish with the slice of orange and remaining cherry.

Amaretto Brandy Rocks

Refreshing and a bit sweet, this cocktail is a nice sipping drink. Enjoy it with spicy appetizers such as jalapeño shrimp dip.

YIELD: 1 SERVING

1 ounce gin
2 teaspoons amaretto
2 teaspoons apricot brandy
Twist of lemon

Partially fill a rocks glass with ice. Add the gin, amaretto, and brandy; stir. Garnish with the lemon twist and serve.

Cognac Rocks with Amaretto

Sit back in front of the fire and enjoy this after-dinner drink. Pecan pie would be a delicious accompaniment.

YIELD: 1 SERVING

1 ounce cognac
½ ounce amaretto

Partially fill a rocks glass with ice. Add the cognac and amaretto. Stir and serve immediately.

Brandy Cream

Serve this as a stand-alone after-dinner drink as you enjoy conversation around the fire, or at the table with chocolate cake.

YIELD: 1 SERVING

1 1/2 ounces brandy
3/4 ounce half-and-half
2 teaspoons simple syrup (sidebar, page 44)

Partially fill a rocks glass with ice. Add the brandy, half-and-half, and sugar syrup. Stir and then serve immediately.

White Russian

I enjoy this as an after-dinner drink, a perfect ending to a delicious meal. Kahlúa is the traditional coffee liqueur used in this drink.

YIELD: 1 SERVING

1 ounce vodka
3/4 ounce coffee liqueur
2 teaspoons half-and-half

Partially fill a rocks glass with ice and add the vodka and coffee liqueur; stir. Float the half-and-half on the top by pouring it over the back of a bar spoon. Serve immediately.

Black Russian

This is basically the same as a White Russian but without the cream. Kahlúa is the preferred liqueur.

Yield: 1 serving

1 1/2 ounces vodka
3/4 ounce coffee liqueur

Partially fill a rocks glass with ice and add the vodka and coffee liqueur. Stir and serve immediately.

Godfather

You may use Scotch, bourbon, or blended whiskey for this classic after-dinner drink. Variations include the Godmother (made with vodka instead of Scotch) and the Godson (made with gin instead of Scotch).

Yield: 1 serving

1 1/2 ounces Scotch
1/2 ounce amaretto

Partially fill a rocks glass with ice and add the Scotch and amaretto. Stir and serve immediately.

"On the rocks," or "rough," refer to wine or distilled spirits that are served over ice in a rocks glass.

Sambuca Up

I had my first Sambuca at the home of Joseph Angello and Bunnie Day when they lived on the Delta just south of Sacramento. This traditional Italian after-dinner drink is served with three coffee beans in the bot-

tom of a cordial glass. The coffee beans signify life, love, and good fortune.

YIELD: 1 SERVING

3 espresso coffee beans
1½ ounces Sambuca

Place the coffee beans in the bottom of a cordial glass and add the Sambuca. Serve and sip slowly.

Blender Drinks

Blender drinks are usually associated with summertime—icy drinks to cool you down on a hot day. There are, however several cozy winter favorites that call the blender into service. The electric blender is used for these drinks as the ingredients are not easy to combine in the standard cocktail shaker, and the ice needs to be incorporated into the finished beverage.

Creamy Ruby Port

Many people contend that milk settles the stomach after a meal. This is a lightly spirited way to enjoy it. You can prepare multiple servings, depending on the capacity of your blender.

YIELD: 1 SERVING

¹/₂ cup cracked ice
³/₄ cup whole milk
3 ounces ruby port
1 teaspoon superfine sugar
Freshly grated nutmeg

Place the ice in a blender, and add the milk, port, and sugar. Pulse briefly to blend. Strain into a collins glass, and then dust with grated nutmeg; serve immediately.

Ramos Fizz

There are many versions of the fizz, but I prefer the one that Paul Bennett prepares. Sunday brunch with friends presents the perfect occasion to serve this drink.

YIELD: 1 SERVING

1¹/₂ ounces gin
1¹/₂ ounces sweet and sour mix
2 ounces orange juice
2 teaspoons sugar
Heaping tablespoon vanilla ice cream
1 egg white
1 cup crushed ice
Slice of orange
Pinch of nutmeg

A fizz made with an egg white is also known as the classic Silver Fizz; when made with an egg yolk it is called a Golden Fizz; and when made with a whole egg it is called a Royal Fizz.

Place the gin, sweet and sour mix, orange juice, sugar, ice cream, and egg white in a blender. Add the crushed ice, and whirl to combine. Pour into a chilled collins glass, and garnish with the orange slice and a pinch of nutmeg. Serve immediately with a straw.

Gold Cadillac

This is an elegant blended drink, usually served in a stemmed cocktail glass.

Yield: 1 serving

2 ounces Galliano
1 ounce white crème de cacao
2 ounces half-and-half
3/4 cup crushed ice

Place the Galliano, crème de cacao, and half-and-half in a blender. Add the ice and blend until smooth. Pour into a chilled cocktail or other fancy glass. Serve immediately.

Hot Spirited Drinks

There is no disputing that a hot drink—spirited or not—will warm your soul. Some of these drinks are classics, some are coffee-based favorites, and others are modern mixes. You will need an espresso machine to prepare many of them, but most are easy to make with standard bar equipment. Ingredients are given to yield a single serving, but as with other drinks in this chapter, the recipes are easy to multiply. These drinks should be served in a brandy snifter or a hot drink mug.

Guy's Hot Buttered Rum with Nutmeg

In the cabin after a day on the ski slopes, hot buttered rum really hits the spot. My husband, Guy Hadler, has prepared this delicious version over the years.

Yield: 1 serving

1 tablespoon brown sugar
4 ounces boiling water
2 ounces dark rum
6-inch cinnamon stick
Scant pat of butter
Freshly grated nutmeg

Place the sugar in the bottom of a warm mug and add a bit of the boiling water. Use the muddler at the end of your bar spoon to mix the sugar with the water until it dissolves. Add the rum and the remaining boiling water. Stir with the cinnamon stick. Place the butter on top and sprinkle with the grated nutmeg. Serve immediately.

Hot Buttered Rum

There are several commercially produced hot buttered rum mixes available, and they make the basis for an excellent drink instantly. On the West Coast, Dan Good brand is widely available, but Trader Vic's is common everywhere. Serve this drink before you go Christmas caroling to improve your voice and to warm your soul.

YIELD: 1 SERVING

1 tablespoon hot buttered rum mix
4 ounces hot water
1 ounce rum
6-inch cinnamon stick

Place the hot buttered rum mix in the bottom of a warm snifter and add the hot water and rum. Stir with the cinnamon stick and serve immediately.

Hot Apple Pie

Tuaca is an apricot liqueur from Italy with a unique flavor. You can easily serve this as the theme drink for a party. Heat the apple cider and keep it warm on the stove or in a heatproof container such as a Crock-Pot or thermal container. Add the Tuaca as you serve each drink.

YIELD: 1 SERVING

4 ounces hot apple cider
1 1/2 ounces Tuaca
6-inch cinnamon stick

Twist of lemon

Pour the hot apple cider into a warm snifter. Add the Tuaca and stir with the cinnamon stick. Garnish with a twist of lemon and serve immediately.

White Nun

We all need calcium, and a nightcap is an excellent way to get some. The fragrance from the hazelnut and herb-based liqueur is soothing.

YIELD: 1 SERVING

4 ounces milk
1 1/2 ounces Frangelico

Steam the milk with an espresso machine according to the directions on page 105. Pour the steamed milk into a warm brandy snifter and stir in the Frangelico. Dot with a bit of the froth from the steaming pitcher and serve immediately.

A Beautiful

This is an elegant and warming after-dinner drink. You may use brandy in place of the cognac, if you wish.

YIELD: 1 SERVING

3/4 ounce cognac
3/4 ounce Grand Marnier
1 1/2 ounces hot water

Twist of lemon

Combine the cognac and Grand Marnier in a warm snifter. Add the hot water and stir to combine. Garnish with the lemon twist and serve immediately.

Nutty Irishman

Two of the ingredients for this drink are nut-based liqueurs: Frangelico from hazelnuts and amaretto from sweet and bitter almonds. This version was first made at Lord Beaverbrooks, a popular fern bar in Sacramento during 1970s.

Yield: 1 serving

4 ounces milk
3/4 ounce Bailey's Irish Cream
1/2 ounce Frangelico
1/2 ounce amaretto

Steam the milk with an espresso machine according to the directions on page 105. Pour the steamed milk into a warm brandy snifter and stir in the Bailey's Irish Cream, Frangelico, and amaretto. Dot with a bit of the froth from the steaming pitcher and serve immediately.

Classic Irish Coffee

I remember the St. Patrick's Day I had my first Irish coffee. I was in college, and a group of us went to some of the local Irish bars to celebrate the occasion. We indulged in a green beer or two and ended the evening with this coffee. Over the years, I have enjoyed this classic recipe many times.

YIELD: 1 SERVING

1 1/2 ounces Irish whiskey
1 teaspoon simple syrup (sidebar, page 44)
4 ounces brewed hot black coffee
1 tablespoon heavy cream

Place the whiskey and sugar syrup in a warm mug or Paris goblet. Add the coffee. Float the heavy cream over the back of a spoon onto the coffee. Serve immediately.

Café Kahlúa with a Tequila Back

This coffee is for the die-hard tequila drinker! Try a specialty blend of coffee such as Guatemala Antigua.

YIELD: 1 SERVING

4 ounces brewed hot black coffee
1 ounce Kahlúa
Pinch of ground cinnamon
1/2 ounce gold tequila

Place the coffee in a warm mug and add the Kahlúa and cinnamon. Stir to combine. Serve immediately with the tequila on the side, in a shot glass.

Keokee Coffee

This is a good drink to serve when you have friends over for a serious game of cards. It will stimulate your conversation and keep you awake.

YIELD: 1 SERVING

3/4 ounce brandy
3/4 ounce Kahlúa
4 ounces brewed hot French roast coffee

Place the brandy and Kahlúa in a warm mug. Stir to combine. Add the coffee, stir, and serve immediately.

Jamaica Coffee

This lovely tropical island has its own signature style of beverages and cooking. The influences of the early European explorers enhanced the local fare.

YIELD: 1 SERVING

1 ounce Jamaican rum
1/2 ounce Tia Maria
4 ounces brewed hot French roast coffee
Generous tablespoon whipped cream
Pinch of ground ginger

Place the rum and Tia Maria in a warm mug. Stir to combine. Add the coffee and top with the whipped cream. Sprinkle with ground ginger.

Café Roma

In Rome, locals frequently enjoy espresso any time of the day. However, after dinner, if not enjoying Sambuca, they might enjoy a hot coffee drink to settle the stomach after a rich meal.

Yield: 1 serving

4 ounces brewed hot Italian roast coffee
1 ounce amaretto
1/2 ounce cognac
Generous tablespoon whipped cream
Pinch of freshly grated nutmeg

Place the coffee and amaretto in a warm mug. Pour the cognac over the back of a spoon to float it on top. Spoon the whipped cream on top of the coffee and then dust with the nutmeg. Serve immediately.

Coffee is common man's gold, and, like gold, it brings to every man the feeling of luxury and nobility.

—Abd-al-Kadir, 1587

Venice-Style Coffee

Venice in the springtime is lovely, but the nights remind you of how cold it is there in the winter months. This amaretto coffee will soothe you, morning or evening.

YIELD: 1 SERVING

4 ounces brewed hot dark roast coffee
1 ounce amaretto
2 tablespoons steamed milk

Pour the brewed coffee into a warm mug. Add the amaretto and stir to blend. Pour the steamed milk over the back side of a spoon into the mug to float it on top. Serve immediately.

Schnapps Hot Chocolate with Mint

Schnapps always reminds me of skiing. There is something about the intense, yet velvety, flavor that complements the cold mountain air. This is a good drink with which to either begin or end a day on the slopes!

YIELD: 1 SERVING

1 tablespoon unsweetened Dutch process cocoa powder
1 teaspoon sugar
1 cup cold low-fat milk
1½ ounces peppermint schnapps
Generous tablespoon whipped cream
Sprig of fresh mint

Place the cocoa and sugar in the bottom of a large warm mug. Steam the milk with an espresso machine according to the directions beginning on page 105. Pour about ¼ cup of the hot steamed milk into the mug and stir to dissolve the cocoa and sugar. Fill the cup with the remaining milk and schnapps and then stir again. Top with the whipped cream. Garnish with the mint and serve immediately.

Hot Chocolate with Frangelico

Frangelico is an amber-colored liqueur that is made from hazelnuts, herbs, and berries. It is a delicious after-dinner drink. Here it is served in frothed hot chocolate. Pass a plate of freshly baked Sandies, the classic ball-shaped cookie that is rolled in confectioners' sugar.

YIELD: 1 SERVING

1 tablespoon unsweetened Dutch process cocoa powder
1 tablespoon simple syrup (sidebar, page 44)
1 teaspoon vanilla syrup
1 cup cold low-fat milk
1 1/2 ounces Frangelico

Place the cocoa, sugar syrup, and vanilla syrup in the bottom of a warm mug and mix into a paste. Steam the milk with an espresso machine according to the directions beginning on page 105. Pour about 1/4 cup of the hot steamed milk into the mug and stir to combine with the cocoa mixture. Fill the cup with the remaining milk and Frangelico and then stir again. Spoon on the froth and serve immediately.

Cancun-Style Hot Cocoa

It does get a bit chilly in the tropics during the winter months, so locals and visitors do enjoy warm drinks. If you cannot get away, gather some friend to look at photos from your past trip and enjoy planning the next adventure over a warm and cozy drink inspired by the region.

YIELD: 1 SERVING

1 cup low-fat milk
1 teaspoon powdered Mexican chocolate
1 teaspoon superfine sugar
1 ounce tequila
1/2 ounce Triple Sec
Generous tablespoon whipped cream

Heat the milk in a small saucepan. Place the chocolate and sugar in a warm mug. Add about 1/4 cup of the hot milk and whisk until creamy and smooth. Add the remaining milk, tequila and Triple Sec. Stir to combine. Top with the whipped cream and serve immediately.

Oolong Tea with Rum and Fresh Bay Leaves

Enjoy this light spirited tea after a poetry reading or at a book club meeting. This recipe is easy to translate into multiple servings. I have a bay laurel tree and so have easy access to the fresh leaves. If you do not have any growing near you, consider planting one, even if only in a large pot. The fresh leaves are mellow, yet distinctively aromatic with the essence of bay.

6 ounces brewed oolong tea
1 medium fresh bay leaf
1 teaspoon honey
1 ounce gold rum
Slice of fresh lemon

Place the brewed tea, bay leaf, and honey in a small saucepan.
Heat over medium heat to dissolve the honey. Add the rum
and then pour into a warm mug. Garnish with the lemon
slice. Serve immediately.

Tea and Sympathy

*I am not sure where the name for this cozy drink originated, but it offers
comfort and warms the soul.*

YIELD: 1 SERVING

4 ounces brewed black tea
1 1/2 ounces Grand Marnier
Twist of lemon

Pour the tea into a warm snifter or mug and stir in the
Grand Marnier. Garnish with the twist of lemon and serve
immediately.

Hot Lemon and Honey

This time-tested mix eases a sore throat. I seldom get sick, but when I do, this comes to the rescue as a bedtime beverage. Curl up in a warm bed with a good book and sip slowly.

YIELD: 1 SERVING

4 ounces hot water
2 ounces freshly squeezed lemon juice
1 ounce brandy
1 tablespoon honey

Place the hot water in a warm mug. Add the lemon juice, brandy, and honey. Stir to combine.

Punches and Mulled Wine

Some occasions call for party-size recipes, and that is when a punch or mulled wine is the appropriate offering. If you are serving a cold punch, place a block of ice or an ice mold in the punch bowl because ice cubes will melt too fast and dilute the mix. When serving mulled beverages make sure they are hot, not lukewarm, as the beverage will cool rapidly if the mugs are set out at room temperature. You can keep the mulled beverage hot in a stockpot over a low heat, or in an electric Crock-Pot. When gauging how much of a beverage to make for a gathering, figure on two to three 5-ounce servings per guest. Get out your grandmother's punch bowl and mugs, and put them to use!

Cranberry-Orange Champagne Punch

This blend has a pinkish color, but do not let that stop you from serving it at a wintertime holiday gathering, or even an afternoon football or basketball party.

YIELD: ABOUT 36 SERVINGS

1/4 cup warm honey
1 cup pure cranberry juice
1 cup freshly squeezed orange juice
1/2 cup freshly squeezed lemon juice
2 limes, thinly sliced
4 fifths (750 ml. each) champagne or sparkling wine, chilled
28-ounce bottle sparkling mineral water, chilled
1 cup orange curaçao, chilled

In a small bowl, stir together the honey, cranberry juice, orange juice, and lemon juice. Add the lime slices, cover, and refrigerate for 3 to 4 hours before serving so the flavors can blend. Just before serving, pour this mixture over a block of ice into a large punch bowl. Add the champagne, mineral water, and orange curaçao. Stir gently to combine. Serve in punch cups, champagne glasses, or wine glasses.

There, gentlemen, is my Champagne and my claret. I am no great judge of the wine and I give you these on the authority of my wine merchant; but I can answer for my punch, for I made it myself.
—Lord Pembroke

Crème de Cassis Champagne Punch

This is a great Christmas morning brunch punch. It comes together quickly and is very festive. Prechill all of the ingredients the night before so that the preparation is quick and effortless.

YIELD: ABOUT 24 SERVINGS

10 ounces fresh black currants or blueberries, rinsed
1/2 cup crème de cassis
1 fifth (750 ml.) sauvignon blanc
2 fifths (750 ml. each) dry champagne or sparkling wine

Place half of the currants in a bowl and add the crème de cassis and sauvignon blanc. Cover and refrigerate for 3 to 4 hours, or overnight. Strain the mixture into a punch bowl over a block of ice and add the remaining currants and champagne. Stir gently to combine. Serve in punch cups, champagne glasses, or wine glasses.

Hot Spiced Merlot

The fragrance fills the air, welcoming your guests. Serve with Jarlsberg cheese, baguette slices, and mixed nuts.

YIELD: ABOUT 12 SERVINGS

2 cups water
1/2 cup honey
1 orange, thinly sliced
1 lemon, thinly sliced

2 1-inch cinnamon sticks
1 tablespoon whole cloves
1 teaspoon freshly grated nutmeg
2 fifths (750 ml. each) merlot

Place the water, honey, orange slices, and lemon slices in a saucepan. Add the cinnamon sticks. Tie the cloves in a square of cheesecloth and add to the pan along with the nutmeg. Heat over medium-low heat for about 1 hour. Strain the mixture into another pan, discarding the orange and lemon slices along with the spices. Add the merlot and heat over medium-low heat. Make sure that you do not boil the mixture. Serve in punch mugs or wine glasses.

Apple brandy that is produced in the United States is called applejack.

Mulled Cider with Calvados

The chill of the early fall weather brings this drink to the table. The aroma sets the mood for autumn foods such as pumpkin soup and apple pie. Serve this cider at a pumpkin-carving party. You may want to make a batch for the children as well—simply omit the calvados.

YIELD: ABOUT 20 SERVINGS

1 gallon apple juice
³/₄ cup freshly squeezed orange juice
¹/₄ cup freshly squeezed lemon juice
¹/₄ cup honey
3 bay leaves
1 6-inch stick cinnamon

6 whole cloves
1 1/2 cups calvados

Pour the apple juice into a large pan and add the orange juice, lemon juice, and honey. Tie the bay leaves, cinnamon stick, and cloves in a large square of cheesecloth and add to the pan. Heat over medium-low heat for about 30 minutes. Remove the spices and add the calvados. Serve in warm mugs.

4

INGREDIENTS FOR COFFEE AND COCOA DRINKS

Fresh, premium-quality beans are essential for brewing an excellent cup of coffee or espresso. Try to purchase your beans directly from a roaster or high-traffic coffee retailer to ensure optimum freshness. Specialty grocers and import stores will supply the widest variety of cocoas. They usually come packaged in a tin and should be stored in a cool, dry place—68 to 78 degrees F is ideal. These ingredients are the base for many hot, cozy drinks.

Coffee

People are passionate about their coffee. Perhaps the unique legendary history surrounding it owes to our ardor. Popular legend has it that ingesting coffee was first discovered by Kaldi, an Ethiopian goat herder, who found his flock frolicking one day among unusual green shrubs bearing red berries. Struck by their level of activity, Kaldi collected some of the berries and took them to a nearby monastery. The monks took great interest and prepared a beverage by boiling the berries—thus the first coffee beverage was created.

Coffee beans found their way to Arabia, and by the thirteenth century the Arabs were roasting and grinding the precious bean and then boiling it with water to produce a

About four thousand hand-picked beans are used to make a single pound of specialty coffee.

beverage. Treasuring their find, the Arabs forbade removal of the raw beans from the country. Their efforts were in vain—by the 1500s raw coffee beans had been smuggled into Turkey, Egypt, and Syria. European traders were introduced to this new stimulating beverage in local coffeehouses. They soon carried coffee to the new colonies throughout the world, where it thrives to this day. Coffee plantations are located throughout the world in countries that lie within the tropical and subtropical zones. These regions are located roughly 100 miles north and south of the equator between the Tropic of Cancer and the Tropic of Capricorn.

Types of Coffee Beans

Arabica and robusta are the two species of coffee plants that grow throughout the world, giving us a myriad of unique coffee beans. Within any given tropical coffee-growing region, unique microclimates contribute to the particular qualities found in the coffee bean. Even within the same growing region, the identical variety of plant will produce a bean with a unique character—much like a vine-yard will yield its signature grapes. The roastmaster, like the winemaker, uses his alchemy to produce a distinct finished product.

Arabica Beans   These beans derive their name from Arabia—the ancient name for Yemen—where they are believed to have originated. These mountain-grown beans thrive in altitudes between 2,000 and 6,000 feet and produce about 75 percent of the world's coffee. This species is grown predominately in Central America, South America, eastern Africa, and Indonesia. All specialty coffees come from arabica beans.

Robusta Beans   This variety of beans grows at elevations between sea level and 2,000 feet and flourishes in wet valley lands and humid tropical forests. Most of the plantations are located in West Africa and Indonesia. Robusta beans have about twice the caffeine content of arabica, and most are used to produce instant coffee or commercial blends.

Types of Coffee Roast

The degree of roast can be broken down into basic categories. Although there is no standard terminology used throughout the industry, these categories will help you understand the flavor differences. Decisions about how quickly and how darkly to roast are in the hands of the roastmaster.

(Coffee is) ... the most precious of bliss's.

—Johann Sebastian Bach

Interestingly enough, darker roast coffees have slightly less caffeine than the lighter roasts because the longer the beans are roasted, the more moisture is removed. Caffeine is part of that moisture and accounts for the oily surface of the beans. An espresso does not contain more caffeine than a cup of commercially roasted coffee, but it does have a stronger, more intense flavor.

Light Roast   Lightly roasted coffees are cinnamon in color and characteristically have intense aromas, with crisp acidity and sourness as the dominant flavor note. They tend to have a light, undeveloped body. Most commercially canned coffee is lightly roasted.

Medium Roast   Medium-roast beans—also known as "city" or "full city"—are chestnut in color and have a perfect balance of body and acidity. The beans' distinguishing characteristics are prevalent. This roast brings out the full range of flavors and is used by most specialty roastmasters.

Dark Roast   In this roast the beans are, as the name implies, a dark bittersweet chocolate brown in color and have a subtle trace of oil on the surface with a slightly roasty bitterness and pungent flavor. The varietal characteristics

are masked, emphasizing this bolder, smoky taste. Espresso and Italian roast fall into this category.

Very Dark Roast   The color of very dark roasted beans is dark brown to black and the surface of the bean is oily. The primary flavor is that of carbony bitterness, without much body. This slightly bitter roast flavor is the most dominant quality of French roast coffee.

Flavor Terminology

The terms used to describe coffee's particular characteristics are similar to those associated with fine wines and are almost endless. The four most important—in addition to the types of roast discussed above—are "aroma," "body," "acidity," and "flavor."

Aroma   This is the fragrance that our senses first detect when presented with freshly brewed coffee. It is distinctive and often complex. The brew may be described as caramel or carbony, fruity or floral, or perhaps herbal or spicy.

Body   "Body" describes how coffee feels on the tongue. It can range from thin and watery, to oily and thick, to buttery or syrupy. This varies depending on the type of bean and brewing method used.

Acidity   The acidity in coffee is not synonymous with bitter or sour and does not refer to its actual acid level—on the pH scale, coffee is relatively low. Rather, it denotes the refreshing, brisk, lively qualities that make coffee a palate-cleansing beverage.

Flavor   *Flavor* is the overall impression and includes the aroma, body, and acidity of the coffee. A particular coffee may be described as having a nutlike aroma, chocolate-like taste, and a smooth, refreshing finish.

Storing Coffee Beans

Fresh premium-quality beans are essential to a great cup of coffee, no matter how you brew it. Unfortunately, roasted coffee beans—whole or ground—have a short shelf life. Moisture, heat, and air cause the flavorful oils and fats in the beans to oxidize after roasting.

Whole beans retain their freshness longer than ground beans because not as much surface area is exposed. Coffee begins to deteriorate within a few hours of being ground but remains mostly unaffected for about a week. The aroma is the first thing that disappears, followed by some of the flavor. Although drinkable, the coffee will lack its unique characteristics. Experts recommend purchasing whole beans in small

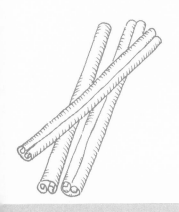

quantities and using them within two to three weeks. Store whole beans—or, if you must, ground coffee—in an airtight container in a cool, dark place. Coffee may be stored in the freezer for longer periods; however, do not take the coffee in and out of the freezer. This causes condensation to build up on the beans, which destroys the flavor of the coffee.

For the ultimate cup, seek out a coffee retailer who also roasts their own beans and make a point of visiting them weekly for your coffee purchases. Grind your coffee at home immediately before brewing it.

Specific Regional Characteristics

There are many coffee beans available from specialty coffee retailers. Coffee beans—like wine grapes—develop certain characteristics specific to the region in which they grow. The soil, sun, and rain all interplay to affect the flavors and body of the bean. Some specific guidelines will help you select coffees to brew at home for cozy drinks.

The Americas   Beans from the Americas tend to be light to medium in body, with a clean and lively flavor. Some of the more popular include Brazil Santos, Colombia Supremo, Guatemala Antigua, Kona, and Mexico Altura.

Coffee is big business; it is second only to oil as a commodity on world markets.

Brazil Santos

Brazil is the world's largest coffee producer; the industry began there in the early 1720s. The beans are generally processed by the dry method. The resulting light-bodied coffee is dry and mildly acidic with a sweet-tasting finish.

Colombia Supremo

Jesuit missionaries first brought coffee to Colombia in 1808, and legend has it that Father Romero encouraged his flock to plant the trees as a form of penance. Today, Colombia is the world's second largest coffee producer. Columbian beans yield a mildly aromatic coffee that has a smooth caramel taste. Medium bodied and nicely balanced, it is also used in many coffee blends.

Guatemala Antigua

Grown in the high elevations of the Antigua region, this coffee is very aromatic, with a dry, nutty flavor and mild texture. It is considered by many to be the best of the Central American varieties.

Kona

King Kamehameha II brought the first coffee plant to the Hawaiian Islands in 1827 after a visit to England. Intended

to be ornamental, the plant thrived in the volcanic soil, giving rise to the industry. The Kona coast on the big island of Hawaii—and more recently parts of Kauai—are the only places in the United States that commercially produce coffee. Grown on the slopes of Mauna Loa and Hualalai volcanoes, Kona coffee is delicately aromatic, mild in flavor, and well balanced.

Mexican Altura

This coffee is grown in southern Mexico on the high slopes of the Sierras. The fragrant aroma, hazelnut flavor, and light body make this well-balanced coffee delicious for breakfast with cream and sugar.

East Africa and Yemen   East Africa and Yemen produce beans that have a sparkling acidity with floral, fruity, or winy flavor notes and a medium to full body. Ethiopia Sidamo, Kenya AA, and Mocha are my favorite coffees from this region.

Ethiopia Sidamo

Arabica coffee is native to Ethiopia. Sidamo is the high plateau growing district in the south-central area of the country. The beans are blue green in color before roasting and yield a coffee that is low acid and full bodied, with a floral aroma and sumptuous aftertaste.

Kenya AA

Many of the beans grown in Africa are the low-elevation robusta variety, but this arabica coffee is grown high on the slopes of Mt. Kenya. The "AA" designation refers to the size of the bean—AA is the largest, followed by A and B grade. Kenya coffee has a ripe blackberry aroma, with a dry winy taste, crisp acidity, and medium-bodied richness.

Mocha

This coffee is organically grown in the mountains of Yemen, much as it was over a thousand years ago. It gained its name from the ancient port of Mocha through which it was originally shipped. Mocha is a distinctive coffee with a light winy acidity and a rich chocolaty aftertaste. This balanced coffee is frequently blended with Java, a bean from Indonesia.

Indonesia　Coffees grown in Indonesia are usually full bodied but smooth, and low in acidity. Their flavor is described as earthy and exotic. These coffees are delicious with milk or cream. Look for Celebes, Java, or Sumatra Mandheling.

Celebes

This low-acid, highly aromatic coffee is named for the former Dutch colony that was located on the small island of Sulawesi, where it is grown. Considered one of the world's finest coffees, it is in short supply and commands a high price. The coffee is characterized by its smooth, rich, slightly smoky taste, a full body, and a sweet finish.

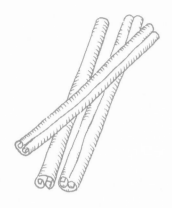

Java

The Dutch first planted coffee trees on the island of Java in 1696, and to this day the word "java" is synonymous with coffee. This full, rich-bodied coffee with nicely balanced acid and complex spicy aroma is delicious on its own, but you will frequently find it blended with the African Mocha bean.

Sumatra Mandheling

This coffee is grown high in the mountains of west-central Sumatra, near the port of Padang. Its herbal aroma, extremely full body, heavy rich flavor, and gentle acidity make it my personal favorite.

Chocolate and Cocoa

It is believed that the jungles of the Amazon produced the first cocoa trees. Centuries ago, the trees were transported to the Yucatán peninsula by the Mayans, who cultivated cocoa as a crop. Cocoa was also a part of Mayan and Aztec mystical and religious rituals. The legend of cocoa, however, really begins with the Aztec emperor Montezuma. History documents that Montezuma drank a chocolate elixir—mixed with herbs and pepper—from golden goblets before retiring to his harem. Perhaps this is how chocolate first gained its reputation as an aphrodisiac.

In 1519 Hernando Cortés, the explorer from Spain, was treated by Montezuma to lavish banquets. He took great interest in this mysterious beverage, as well as the golden, jeweled goblets in which it was served. When he returned to Spain in 1528, Cortés took both with him. He served the royal court a sugar-sweetened cocoa beverage that the aristocracy embraced with a passion. In the span of 100 years, cocoa made its way across Europe, and the cocoa plants to plantations throughout the new colonies.

The trees flourish in tropical areas—the cocoa belt—that lies 20 degrees north and south of the equator. Most plantations are located in Africa, South and Central America, and parts of Asia.

Types of Cocoa Plants

Forasteros and criollos are the two basic species of cocoa plants, although many hybrids have been developed. Trinitario is believed to be a natural cross-strain of the criollo and forastero species of cocoa plants. These trees are particularly suitable for cultivation.

In 1492, Columbus presented the court of King Ferdinand with a treasure trove of many strange and wondrous things including a few cocoa beans. However, it was not until 1528, when Cortés returned to Spain, that the potential of cocoa was recognized.

Forasteros   This species grows primarily in West Africa and Brazil. It is a hearty plant that produces thick-walled pods. The cured seeds of this variety are often used by chocolatiers as the base bean and blended with more flavorful varieties.

Criollos   Criollos produce a thin-skinned pod that hosts a seed noted for its concentrated flavor. This delicate plant thrives in Java, Samoa, Venezuela, Sri Lanka, and Madagascar. These beans produce the finest quality products and are noted for their aromatic quality.

Roasting Cocoa Seeds

The pods are harvested, cracked open to expose the seeds, and placed in the sun to ferment. After the pulp ferments away—in two to three days—the seeds are placed in baskets, where they continue to ferment for three to nine days. This fermentation process removes the bitter acid and develops the essential oils, turning the seeds into dark brown beans. These are then dried before they are packaged for shipping.

Dried cocoa beans are stored in warehouses, where they are cleaned and sorted according to size. The various types of beans are then secretly blended to create each manufacturer's unique concoction. The chocolatier then presides over the roasting, determining the temperature and degree of

A cocoa tree sprouts thousands of tiny waxy pink or white blossoms, but only 3 to 10 percent mature into full fruit.

roast. The cocoa beans develop their characteristic aroma, flavor, and color when roasted.

After roasting, the warm beans are placed in a machine that breaks off the outer shells, revealing the nibs—small pieces of the bean that contain 50 to 54 percent cocoa butter. The nibs are crushed between steel or stone disks in a process known as conching. This generates heat, which liquefies the cocoa butter—most of which is removed—yielding the chocolate liquor, a thick dark cocoa paste. This chocolate liquor is the base ingredient from which all other forms of chocolate are made.

Cocoa manufacturers carefully guard the three critical factors in chocolate making: proportions of ingredients, temperatures, and time intervals.

Types of Cocoa and Chocolate and Storing Tips

The amount of cocoa butter in the finished product distinguishes the different types of chocolate. Powdered cocoa and solid-bar chocolate both have distinctive characteristics and specific uses.

Each type of chocolate has slightly different storage requirements. In general, however, chocolate should be stored in a cool, dry place—68 to 78 degrees F is ideal. When stored at cold temperatures, such as in the refrigerator or freezer, chocolate will sweat when brought to room temperature. In too warm a temperature, the chocolate will develop a pale color on its exterior—a bloom. This happens when a slight

amount of the cocoa butter separates and rises to the surface. The chocolate itself is not spoiled, just its appearance. Recipes in this book call for the use of chocolate syrup, cocoa powder, or unsweetened chocolate.

Chocolate Syrup   Chocolate syrup is cocoa powder, water, granulated sugar, salt, and vanilla. Hershey's makes excellent chocolate syrup and, refrigerated, it will keep indefinitely.

Cocoa Powder   This is pulverized chocolate liquor. Most of the cocoa butter has been pressed out during processing, yielding a product containing only 10 to 24 percent cocoa butter. It is convenient to use in baking or beverages since it does not have to be melted. There are two types of cocoa powder, natural and Dutch process. The natural cocoa powder—meaning nonalkalized—has a strong chocolate flavor and medium brown color. Coenraad van Houten, a Dutchman, invented the Dutching machine, which treats the cocoa with an alkali to neutralize the natural acidity. Most European cocoas are Dutch process. They have a slightly milder flavor and darker chocolate color. Stored in a tin away from moisture, cocoa powder will last for years. I like unsweetened Dutch process cocoa powder for cozy drinks.

Unsweetened Chocolate   Sometimes called baking chocolate, unsweetened chocolate is chocolate liquor that has been molded into blocks and hardened. It contains no sugar and thus has a bitter taste. The content of cocoa butter in this form of chocolate ranges between 50 and 58 percent depending on the blend of cocoa beans used. Unsweetened chocolate is frequently used for making brownies, fudges, frostings, and some hot chocolate drinks. Look for it in packages of eight individually wrapped one-ounce portions. This chocolate will keep indefinitely if stored well wrapped in a cool, dry place.

Flavored Syrups

Sugar syrup and flavored syrups are used to add a special uniqueness to many drinks. It is easy to make homemade sugar syrup (see sidebar, page 44). Several different flavored syrups are on the market, but I like the Torani Italian syrups for their variety, availability, and consistency. Keep some flavors on hand, including caramel, chocolate mint, coconut, crème de cacao, English toffee, hazelnut, Irish cream, mint, orgeat, raspberry, strawberry, toasted walnut, and vanilla.

My figure is the result of a
lifetime of chocolate eating.
—Katharine Hepburn

5

TOOLS AND TECHNIQUES FOR COFFEE AND COCOA DRINKS

Many gadgets designed to produce the perfect cup of coffee or espresso are available in specialty stores. Armed with some knowledge, you can purchase appliances that will meet your needs and satisfy your sense of aesthetics. Most cocoa beverages don't require any special equipment beyond a saucepan, whisk, and blender. There are, however, some techniques that will make brewing coffee and espresso seem effortless and blending cocoa powder and preparing chocolate beverages easier.

Coffee Grinders

The grinding process has evolved throughout the centuries. Early on, the roasted beans were pounded with a mortar and pestle to unlock the flavor within. With the advent of the millstone, the same type of large wheels that were used to grind wheat berries were employed to grind coffee. Today, you can choose hand-crank, electric blade, or burr grinders.

Hand-Crank Grinders

This millstone-type of grinder does not require electricity and can be set for a specific grind, thus producing a consistently ground coffee. With the proper setting you can even grind beans to espresso specifications.

Electric Blade Grinders

These inexpensive grinders are used in most homes. They whirl two blades at a high speed, chopping the beans into irregular pieces. You determine the type of grind by the length of time you whirl the beans around, not by a predetermined setting. Each machine differs slightly, but the following guidelines may be applied.

- ❖ French press plunger pots: coarse grind, about 6 seconds
- ❖ Flat-bottom drip filters: medium grind, about 10 seconds
- ❖ Cone-shaped drip filters: fine grind, about 25 seconds
- ❖ Espresso: extra-fine powderlike grind, 30 or more seconds

Keep your grinder clean. Coffee beans contain oil that leaves a residue, which can cause the next batch of beans that you grind to be bitter. The residue can even clog the machine. Use a stiff brush to remove any coffee from the blades or burrs, and then take a soft cloth to wipe the bean container and lid clean.

It is difficult to produce a grind that is fine enough for espresso with an electric blade grinder, so you may want to have it ground where you purchase your beans. The blades of this type of grinder can generate heat that will adversely affect

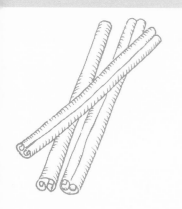

the volatile oils in the beans. To avoid this, grind your beans in spurts, for a few seconds at a time.

Burr Grinders

Although expensive, these grinders produce a uniform grind ranging from coarse to extra fine. The machine is set to a calibrated grade, individually crushing the whole beans. Heat is minimized in the grinding process, leaving the volatile oils undisturbed.

Coffee Brewing Equipment

All brewing equipment has one thing in common—coffee beans come into contact with water to yield a unique beverage. With the correct water temperature and type and grind of coffee, you can produce a perfect cup. Drip, French press, and espresso are the most popular brewing methods, each preparation calling specific equipment into service.

Drip Coffee Makers

This popular method of brewing coffee can be done manually or automatically. In either case, hot water passes through coffee grounds that are held in a paper or wire mesh filter. The coffee drips into a carafe, ready to serve immediately.

French Press

Also known as plunger pot coffee, this is an open-pot brewing method, meaning that the coffee grounds are put directly into a pot of water. In this case, the coffee is put into a narrow glass cylinder that is fitted with a fine mesh screen plunger. Hot water is poured into the pot and allowed to steep with the coffee grounds for about four minutes. The plunger is then slowly pushed down, filtering the coffee as it carries the grounds to the bottom of the pot. This is quite an elegant way to serve coffee to guests at brunch or at a dinner party.

Espresso Machines

Coffee brewed in this manner requires more sophisticated equipment and is a bit more involved than other methods. Hot water is forced under pressure through very finely ground, firmly packed coffee. A vast array of espresso makers are available for a variety of prices. There are three basic categories.

✦ Stovetop machines. These are the least expensive, but they do have their drawbacks. Water is heated in the lower compartment to produce steam pressure, which forces the water into the upper compartment through the grounds. It is difficult to control the water temperature and the amount of water that goes through the grounds.

You often end up with a thin, overextracted, and bitter brew. These machines are not equipped to froth milk.

✧ Electric steam machines. These use steam pressure to force water through the grounds. In most machines of this type the entire amount of water put into the chamber will flow through the brew head. They have a steaming wand, but it is difficult to froth milk since the steam you need dissipates as the water drains through the brew head.

✧ Pump or piston machines. To brew espresso drinks at home that will rival any good coffeehouse version, you need a pump or piston machine. Both types heat the water to the temperature that is required for espresso—192 to 198 degrees F. The pump machines use an electric pump to force water through the grounds; the piston style relies on a hand-operated piston. Easy-to-use milk frothing wands are built in, and a switch activates a separate thermostat to heat the water between 250 and 270 degrees F—the necessary temperature for steaming and frothing milk. The reservoirs in these machines are large enough to hold about 4 cups of water, enough to produce 20 to 25 espresso drinks with frothed milk. Additionally, the reservoir may be refilled while the machine is in use. I use a pump espresso machine and love the results.

Espresso Measure

This is a small stainless steel pitcher that is used to collect the espresso as it drips from the machine. It holds a shot of espresso, usually $1\frac{1}{2}$ ounces.

Frothing Pitcher

This is a stainless steel pitcher with a handle that is used to froth milk. Pitchers come in different sizes, ranging from 10 to 20 ounces.

The Art of the Cup

Think of a tea party with the perfect set of cups. This is what you will want to showcase your cozy coffee and cocoa beverages. Many different colors of ceramic cups and mugs are available—choose ones to suit your style. You may want to have some that are made of glass as well so that you can see the layers of color in the drinks.

Cappuccino Cup

These cups can be ceramic or glass and usually have a saucer. The average size is 5 ounces.

Once you get a mouthful of very hot coffee, whatever you do next is going to be wrong.

—Anonymous

Coffee Cup or Mug

Many shapes and sizes are available to serve mochas, cappuccino, and latte drinks. Have a selection of clear glass as well as ceramic ones. Sizes usually range from 4 to 8 ounces.

Espresso Cup

An espresso cup is a small mug made of either glass or ceramic that is perfect for the single or double shot of espresso. Sizes range from 2 to 3 ounces. Some come with a cute mini saucer.

Latte Cup

This cup is usually ceramic and almost like a small bowl. The average size is 9 ounces.

Soda Fountain Glasses

These old-fashioned footed glasses are perfect for many cocoa and chocolate drinks. They are designed to hold from 8 to 12 ounces. Serve with a straw and long-handled spoon.

Basic Techniques for Preparing Coffee and Espresso Drinks

There are a few techniques that will make preparation a joy. Have your coffee, specialty ingredients, necessary tools, and

If you are pouring a hot drink into a cold glass or mug, place a metal spoon in the glass, which will absorb the heat and prevent the glass from breaking.

serving cups (preheated) set out before you begin to brew the coffee.

Drip Coffee

Purchase freshly roasted beans, and, if possible, grind them just before brewing. Use 2 tablespoons of ground coffee (one standard measure) for every 6 ounces of cold water. Always use fresh water. Depending on the quality of your tap water, you may wish to use filtered or bottled water. The water temperature should be just below boiling, 195 to 205 degrees F. Automatic drip brewers have a built-in thermostat to regulate the water temperature. If you are using a drip cone system, be sure to pour the measured amount of water through just before it comes to a boil. If it does boil, allow the water to cool a bit before adding it to the machine.

Helpful Tips for Drip Coffee   The following tips will help you achieve a delicious pot of coffee every time.

✦ Unbleached paper coffee filters are more environmentally friendly than bleached white filters. Better yet, purchase a gold-coated filter. It is made of a high-density plastic that is coated with 23-karat gold. To clean, simply discard the wet grounds and use a sponge and mild soap to wash the filter. Do not put it in the dishwasher, as this washing method will wear away the gold plating.

✧ Too fine a grind causes a bitter brew as the water is in contact with the surface area of the beans for too long. Too coarse a grind causes a watery coffee because the water passes through the grounds too rapidly.

✧ Do not reuse coffee grounds. The delicious flavors are extracted in the initial brewing process, leaving grounds that will yield a bitter brew the second time around.

✧ Too low a water temperature causes underextraction. The flavor compounds don't dissolve completely, and the resulting coffee is weak. Too high a water temperature can actually burn the coffee, causing an unpleasant flavor.

✧ Brewed coffee retains its optimum freshness and full flavor for 20 to 30 minutes. Continuous heating on a coffee machine's heating plate causes the coffee to develop a sour and bitter taste.

✧ Thermal containers are the best way to hold coffee for extended periods of time. A temperature of 180 to 190 degrees F is optimal.

If you want to improve your understanding, drink coffee.

—Sydney Smith

French Press Coffee

French press coffee (also known as plunger pot coffee) is an open-pot brewing method that steeps the coffee grounds in hot water. The grounds, which are coarser than those used for drip coffee, are forced to the bottom of the pot by pressing a fine mesh screen through the brew. This press method produces a rich, flavorful drink, bringing out all the qualities of the coffee as the grounds steep in the pot.

As with drip coffee, use 2 tablespoons of coffee per 6 ounces of hot water. The water should be just below boiling, 195 to 205 degrees F. Stir slightly, and then place the plunger assembly loosely on the top to retain the heat. Steep for 4 minutes, and then hold the pot by the handle and slowly press the plunger down through the liquid. The grounds will be carried to the bottom of the pot. Serve immediately.

Helpful Tips for French Press Brewing   The following tips should help while you are learning to use your French press brewing system.

- ❖ Preheat the pot and plunger assembly before adding the coffee and hot water.
- ❖ Do not overfill the pot with water—it will spill out of the spout when you depress the plunger assembly.
- ❖ Clean the pot and plunger with hot soapy water after each use.

Espresso Drinks

Preparing espresso is an art form unto itself. The steps are a ritual, each to be performed in a precise manner. Espresso, properly prepared, is not harsh but rather smooth and aromatic without any bitterness. Crema, the bittersweet creamy foam that tops an espresso, is the signature of a perfectly brewed cup. It occurs only when the right amount of freshly ground espresso beans have had the proper amount of water, at precisely the right temperature, forced through them by the steam of your espresso machine. Once the steps are mastered, you can brew a perfect cup every time.

The grind of the bean is critical. A grind that feels like flour is too fine; it should be more like salt. Water cannot flow through a grind that is too fine, and if it is too coarse, it will flow so fast that the full body of the coffee will not be extracted and the crema will not be produced. Preheat your espresso machine with the filter holder in the brew head. The time required will vary from machine to machine, so get to know how long it takes yours to reach the optimum temperature. This will usually take at least 5 minutes—longer than the actual brewing time.

Remove the filter holder from the brew head and insert the one- or two-serving metal basket. For the one-shot basket, fill with about 1 tablespoon finely ground espresso beans.

A "shot" refers to a measure of alcohol or expresso ranging from 1 to 2 ounces.

Tamp lightly. You want to level the ground beans, not tightly pack them. Wipe any grounds off the edge of the filter holder since they will inhibit a tight seal on the brew head. Follow the same steps when using the two-shot basket, adding 2 table-spoons of ground espresso beans.

Insert the filter holder into the brew head and turn to lock in place. If brewing one shot, place a warm espresso cup or measuring cup under the brew head, making sure that it is properly lined up. For two shots, place the cups side-by-side. Turn the preheated machine to the brewing setting. After about 15 seconds, enough pressure will build up in the brew head and a trickle of dark espresso, followed by the golden crema, will flow into the cup. This will take between 18 and 25 seconds, depending on your machine. Turn off the switch as soon as 1½ ounces—a shot of espresso—has been extracted.

Helpful Tips for Espresso Drinks   Use the following tips to master your espresso maker.

✦ As with any coffee, depending on the quality of your tap water, you may want to use filtered or bottled water.

✦ If the espresso does not come out of the brew head, several things could be wrong. First check the obvious. Make sure there is water in the water reservoir and that

In 1793, a small group of auctioneers and merchants began meeting regularly at the Tontine Coffee House in New York City. Their enterprise eventually became the New York Stock Exchange.

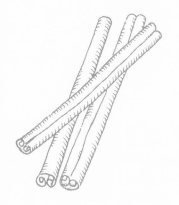

the siphon hose is properly attached. Alternatively, the espresso beans may be too finely ground or tamped too hard, inhibiting the flow of water. Too many grounds in the filter basket could also be the problem.

✦ If the espresso comes out too quickly, the water in the machine may not have reached the proper temperature. Another cause may be beans that are stale or too coarsely ground. Make sure there is enough ground espresso in the filter basket and that it is properly tamped down.

✦ Espresso spurting from where the filter holder is attached to the machine is an indication that it may not be properly locked into place or that the filter holder may not be making a tight enough seal due to grounds being in the way.

✦ If your espresso has a bitter taste, you may have allowed too much water to flow through the filter basket, thereby extracting the bitter oils from the grounds. Allow only 1 1/2 ounces of water per serving to flow through the filter basket. If you do not like a strong espresso, simply dilute it with some hot water from the steam vent.

✦ If your espresso is not hot enough, you may not have allowed the machine to heat up long enough to bring the water to the proper brewing temperature, or you may not have preheated your cups.

- Use hot water to rinse the filter holder and metal espresso grounds basket after each use. Several times a year you may want to clean these thoroughly by soaking them for several hours in a solution of 1 part white vinegar or baking soda to 4 parts water.

- Do not remove the brew head until the pressure has gone down, or you may be burned. Clean the brew head of your espresso machine after each use to prevent an oily residue buildup that will spoil the taste of your next espresso.

- Serve espresso in preheated 2- to 3-ounce demitasse cups, cappuccino in pre-heated 5-ounce cups, and café latte or mocha drinks in 9-ounce cups.

Frothing Milk

Frothing—or steaming—milk is a process that heats milk and creates a head of froth, or foam. When poured atop hot espresso, the froth not only keeps the coffee warm, it provides a surface upon which to shake powdered cocoa or ground cinnamon. Frothing also prevents a skin from forming on the surface of the milk, as happens when milk is heated in a saucepan.

There are two foolproof but completely different techniques for frothing milk. One relies on a microwave oven, the other on an espresso machine with a frothing wand.

❖ To froth milk in a *microwave oven,* pour the desired amount of cold milk into a deep bowl. Place the bowl in the microwave oven and heat for 2 to 3 minutes, depending on the power level of your microwave. Remove when milk is scalded but not boiling. Lower the blades of a hand-crank mixer into the milk and rapidly crank until the milk is airy—frothed.

❖ A pump-driven *espresso machine* will froth milk quickly and effortlessly once you become familiar with the process. These machines have a built-in thermostat to heat the water to one temperature to produce espresso, and another—slightly hotter—to produce the steam required to froth milk.

Each espresso machine will have specific directions in the instruction manual; however, certain procedures are always the same.

1. Thoroughly preheat your machine. A "ready light" will go on or off, depending on the design. I allow mine an extra few minutes for good measure. Place a sponge or empty cup under the steam vent, then open the valve and allow any condensation to clear. This avoids watering down the milk. Close the valve once it's cleared.

2. Add the desired amount of cold milk to a chilled metal pitcher. Since quite a head of froth will build up, be sure that the pitcher is only one-third full.

3. Keep the steam vent just below the surface of the milk, but do not allow it to reach the bottom of the pitcher. Open the steam valve completely. As the milk begins to froth, move the frothing pitcher slightly up and down to incorporate more air. The milk will double in volume. Feel the bottom of the pitcher; it should be hot but not scalding to the touch.

4. Turn the steam vent off before removing the pitcher; otherwise, hot milk will splatter.

Helpful Tips for Frothing Milk   Frothing milk is an elegant touch surrounded by mystery. These tips will help to make this process simple:

✧   Frothing pitchers are available in 10- to 20-ounce sizes. The larger size is necessary for steaming milk for latte, mocha, or steamed hot cocoa drinks. Store the pitcher in the freezer or refrigerator as very cold milk froths the best.

✧   Put cold milk in a cold frothing pitcher just before you are ready to steam it.

❖ When the tip of the frothing wand (steam vent) is correctly placed in the milk, you will hear a hissing sound, the surface of the milk will begin to seethe, and small bubbles will begin to form. If the wand is lowered too deeply into the milk, it will sound more like a rumble, and large bubbles will form.

❖ Frothed milk should be smooth and thick with small bubbles. Large bubbles dissipate too quickly in the finished beverage.

❖ Steamed milk should be present at the bottom of the pitcher; not all of the milk will be transformed into froth. Overheating the milk will destroy the froth.

❖ Warm or stale milk will not froth. Low-fat milk will froth more easily because it contains less butterfat.

❖ Clean your frothing wand after every use. Open the steam vent for several seconds to force out any milk that may have entered it. Then use a damp cloth to wipe the steam vent clean before the milk hardens on it.

❖ If you forget to clean the frothing wand and the milk residue hardens on it, immerse it in a tall glass of hot water and allow it to sit overnight. Wipe it clean in the morning.

◆ Before frothing milk, be sure to allow some steam to run through the wand to clean out any hardened milk.

Basic Techniques for Preparing Cocoa and Chocolate Beverages

Blending the cocoa powder with hot water to form a smooth paste is the most critical element in producing a quality hot or cold cocoa-based drink. For hot drinks, start with a clean saucepan and stir together the cocoa powder and sugar. Whisk in some hot water until a smooth paste has been achieved. Warm over medium heat as you whisk in the cold milk. Do not allow the mixture to come to a boil—remove from the heat when small bubbles begin to form around the edges. Whisk again to froth slightly, then serve steaming hot.

Cold cocoa or chocolate drinks also rely on thoroughly blending the ingredients. A high-quality blender is essential. The blender should not be filled to more than two-thirds of its capacity—you need plenty of headroom for the foam to develop.

Helpful Tips for Cocoa and Chocolate Beverages   Follow these tips when preparing cocoa and chocolate drinks.

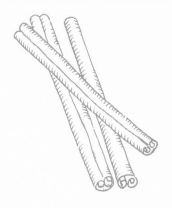

Spain's Princess Maria Theresa made chocolate the rage of Europe when she presented cocoa beans as an engagement gift to King Louis XIV.

- Use unsweetened Dutch process cocoa powder for hot or cold drinks. It has a slightly softer, more delicate flavor.

- Serve hot cocoa drinks in preheated 5- to 6-ounce mugs.

- Chill the blender bucket before preparing cold blended drinks.

- Serve cold cocoa drinks in chilled glasses. Old-fashioned soda fountain glasses are particularly fun.

6

RECIPES FOR COZY COFFEE AND COCOA DRINKS

Young and old alike love coffee and cocoa drinks. They are quick and easy to prepare any time of the day. Finish a cozy wintertime dinner with an Orgeat Cappuccino or Coconut Café Mocha. Serve Milk Frothed with Chocolate and Mint for an early springtime dessert. Snuggle in bed on a cold night with a mug of Orange Spice Hot Chocolate. I like to wrap holiday presents while I enjoy a Yule Latte or Sweet Mexican Mocha. Master the use of your espresso machine as discussed in chapter 5, and you will be a star in your own home.

Hot Brewed Coffee Drinks

The recipes for brewed coffee drinks make several servings at once since standard brewing equipment prepares more than one cup at a time. Many coffee brewing machines are available for home use, exhibiting a wide range of methods and styles. They all achieve the same end—separating the grounds from the coffee as it is brewed. With either manual or electric, precise measurement and water temperature are required.

The standard serving size for a cup of brewed coffee is 6 ounces. To achieve this, start with 1 scoop—equal to 2 table-spoons—of ground coffee beans for each 6 ounces of cold water. See page 99 for helpful tips.

Coconut Kona Coffee

One of my favorite places to spend a few weeks during the cold winter months is Hawaii. Try this recipe to bring the warmth of the islands to your home.

YIELD: 4 SERVINGS

1/2 cup ground Kona coffee
3 cups cold water
1/4 cup coconut syrup

Place the coffee grounds in a filter basket. Add the water and brew the coffee using the automatic drip method. Stir in the coconut syrup, then serve in warm cups.

Brewed Coffee with Cinnamon and Nutmeg

This drink is best made with a medium-bodied coffee such as Mocha Java. The cinnamon and nutmeg are very aromatic, filling the kitchen with a wonderful scent as the coffee brews.

YIELD: 4 SERVINGS

1/2 cup ground medium-bodied coffee
1/4 teaspoon ground cinnamon
Scant 1/8 teaspoon freshly ground nutmeg
3 cups cold water

Place the coffee grounds in a filter basket and sprinkle the cinnamon and nutmeg on top. Add the water and brew the

The plantation that I visited in Kona is on the slopes of Mauna Loa. Mango trees are planted in neat rows to provide shade for the coffee trees. A cup of Kona always takes me back to the islands.

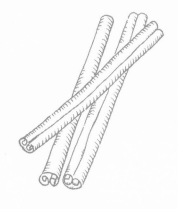

coffee using the automatic drip method. Serve immediately in warm cups.

Crème de Cacao Coffee

This is a wonderful after-dinner coffee. You can have everything pre-measured and ready to go. Serve chocolate mint cookies on the side.

YIELD: 4 SERVINGS

1/2 cup ground French roast coffee
3 cups cold water
2 tablespoons crème de cacao syrup
4 sprigs fresh mint (optional)

Place the coffee grounds in a filter basket. Add the water and brew the coffee using the manual or automatic drip method. Stir in the crème de cacao syrup, and then serve in warm cups. Garnish with the fresh mint if desired.

French Roast Coffee with Vanilla and Cream

Serve this rich, dark French roast coffee with chocolate cake. Indulgent, but so very good!

YIELD: 4 SERVINGS

1/2 cup ground French roast coffee
3 cups cold water
1/4 cup vanilla syrup
3 tablespoons half-and-half

Where coffee is served there is grace and splendor.
—Anonymous

Place the coffee grounds in a filter basket. Add the water and brew the coffee using the automatic drip method. Stir the vanilla syrup and half-and-half into the brewed coffee and serve in warm cups.

Coffee Marsala

The light acidity and slight chocolate aftertaste make Mocha beans the perfect choice for this popular Indian-style coffee. Invite some friends over and serve with gingerbread for a pre-shopping treat.

YIELD: 4 SERVINGS

¹/₂ cup ground Mocha coffee
¹/₈ teaspoon ground cardamom
Several grinds nutmeg
3 cups cold water

Place the coffee grounds in a filter basket and top them with the cardamom and nutmeg. Add the water and brew the coffee using the automatic drip method. Serve immediately in warm cups.

French Press and Open-Pot Coffees

French press coffee makers brew an excellent coffee with a bit of fine sediment that gives the coffee a thick, full-bodied flavor. Remember to use coarse grounds for French press (plunger pot) coffees so that most of the sediment is filtered out. Open-pot brewing is a time-honored technique still popular in many parts of the world. Serve coffee prepared this way after a dinner with an international theme to open up the topic of coffee preparation. Try my recipes, and then create your own variations.

French Press Coffee with Cardamom and Ginger

People who enjoy a dark rich style of coffee will love this recipe. Use an Italian or French roast coffee. Take the Sunday paper to your favorite place in the house and leisurely enjoy the morning.

Yield: 4 servings

3 cups cold water
1/2 cup coarse-ground dark roast coffee
1/8 teaspoon ground cardamom
Pinch of ground ginger
Sugar (optional)

Bring the water to a boil, remove from the heat, and allow it to cool slightly. Place the coffee, cardamom, and ginger in the pot of a French press (plunger pot) coffee maker. Pour in the water and place the plunger assembly on the top, but do not push down on the plunger. Allow coffee to steep for

4 minutes, then slowly press down on the plunger. This will carry the coffee grounds to the bottom of the pot. Serve immediately with sugar, if you like it sweet.

Cinnamon Walnut Coffee

The aroma of cinnamon always calls to mind homemade cinnamon rolls. Serve this coffee with fresh baked or purchased rolls and fruit cups for a wonderful brunch.

YIELD: 4 SERVINGS

3 cups cold water
$1/2$ cup coarse-ground Sumatra roast coffee
$1/4$ teaspoon ground cinnamon
$1/4$ cup toasted walnut syrup

Bring the water to a boil, remove from the heat, and allow it to cool slightly. Place the coffee and cinnamon in the pot of a French press (plunger pot) coffee maker. Pour in the water and place the plunger assembly on the top, but do not push down on the plunger. Allow it to steep for 4 minutes, then slowly press down on the plunger. This will carry the coffee grounds to the bottom of the pot. Place 1 tablespoon of toasted walnut syrup in the bottom of each warm cup and pour in the coffee. Serve immediately.

Parisian-Style French Coffee

When you order French roast coffee in Paris, you will frequently have it served to you in a plunger pot. Try this at home. Place the French press pot on the table and allow people to serve themselves. Be sure to provide warm mugs.

Yield: 4 servings

3 cups cold water
1/2 cup coarse-ground French roast coffee
Sugar (optional)

Bring the water to a boil, remove from the heat, and allow it to cool slightly. Place the coffee in the pot of a French press (plunger pot) coffee maker. Pour in the water and place the plunger assembly on the top, but do not push down on the plunger. Allow coffee to steep for 4 minutes, then slowly press down on the plunger. This will carry the coffee grounds to the bottom of the pot. Serve immediately. Pass the sugar, if desired.

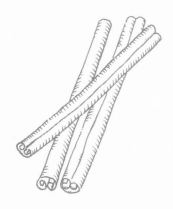

Café de Olla

This is a traditional Mexican coffee drink and is usually prepared in a clay pot. All of the ingredients go directly in the pot and simmer to allow the flavors to marry. If you can find panocha (piloncillo), the cone-shaped brown sugar from Mexico, use 4 small cones in place of the brown sugar.

4 cups cold water
1/2 cup coarsely ground Colombia Supremo roast coffee
1/2 cup firmly packed dark brown sugar
4-inch cinnamon stick
4 whole cloves
Peel of 1/2 orange, sliced

Place the water in a saucepan over high heat and bring it to a boil. Reduce the heat slightly and add the coffee, sugar, cinnamon stick, cloves, and orange peel. Gently simmer for 5 minutes, and then stir in 1/2 cup cold water. Strain the mixture through a paper coffee filter into a warm pot. Serve immediately in warm mugs.

Traditional Middle Eastern Coffee

Many believe that coffee originated in Ethiopia. Open-pot coffee brewing has been used for years in Ethiopia and is still prepared there today in the ibrik. An ibrik is a small conical pot made of copper or brass that is tinned inside. Coffee prepared this way is also referred to as Turkish coffee. Have your coffee retailer finely grind Italian roast beans for you.

YIELD: 2 SERVINGS

4 teaspoons finely ground dark roast coffee
2 tablespoons sugar
Pinch of cardamom (optional)
1/4 cup cold water

Place the coffee and sugar (and cardamom, if desired) in a small saucepan, or in a traditional ibrik. Add the water and heat over medium-high heat. After a few minutes the coffee will begin to gently boil. A darkish crust will form on the top of the foam as it works its way up the sides of the saucepan or ibrik. Watch it closely—you do not want the pot to overflow. Slowly pour into demitasse cups, taking care that the foam does not settle.

Espresso Drinks

Espresso has been popular in Europe since the early 1900s but has just won the hearts of Americans within the last 20 or so years. Today, most of us would not think of starting the day without our favorite espresso, latte, or mocha. Many excellent home brewing espresso machines are available, bringing the easy preparation of this invigorating beverage directly into our kitchens. See general tips for brewing espresso and frothing milk beginning on page 105. Since each espresso machine is slightly different, be sure to consult your instruction manual.

These recipes are given as single servings since many espresso machines brew only one shot (usually $1\frac{1}{2}$ ounces) at a time. All of the ingredients are easy to multiply, so making additional servings is easy.

Hazelnut Espresso

Slightly sweet and nutty, this espresso is delicious. Most often espresso is served black or with a twist of lemon or a lump of sugar. This version is sweetened with hazelnut syrup and has a float of cream on top.

YIELD: 1 SERVING

1 shot espresso
1 teaspoon hazelnut syrup
1 teaspoon heavy cream

Pour the brewed espresso into a small, warm espresso cup. Stir in the hazelnut syrup, and then pour the cream over the back side of a spoon to float it on top. Serve immediately.

Chocolate Mint Espresso

Chocolate, mint, and coffee all in one little demitasse cup—this is a delicious finish to a meal.

YIELD: 1 SERVING

1 shot espresso
1 teaspoon chocolate mint syrup
1/2 teaspoon granulated sugar

Pour the brewed espresso into a small, warm espresso cup. Stir in the chocolate mint syrup and sugar. Serve immediately.

Irish Cream Espresso

This espresso drink is as delicious as traditional Irish coffee, but without the alcohol.

YIELD: 1 SERVING

1 shot espresso
1 teaspoon Irish cream syrup
1/2 teaspoon granulated sugar

Pour the brewed espresso into a small, warm espresso cup. Stir in the Irish cream syrup and the granulated sugar. Serve immediately.

Almond Mocha Latte

Frothed milk laced with espresso and rich flavors is such a delightful way to get your calcium. Serve this with almond cookies and mocha ice cream for an afternoon treat.

YIELD: 1 SERVING

1 shot espresso
1 teaspoon orgeat syrup
1 teaspoon crème de cacao syrup
1/3 cup cold low-fat milk

Pour the brewed espresso into a warm 5-ounce mug. Stir in the orgeat syrup and the crème de cacao syrup. Place the milk

Fruit- and nut-flavored syrups are used in many recipes throughout this book. These presweetened extracts are available in many coffee shops and specialty markets. Popular brands are Torani and Monin.

in a cold frothing pitcher and steam. Pour the steamed milk over the espresso, and spoon the froth in top. Serve immediately.

Pour the brewed espresso into a warm 9-ounce mug. Stir in the strawberry syrup. Place the milk in a cold frothing pitcher and steam. Pour the steamed milk over the espresso, and spoon the froth on top. Serve immediately.

Yule Latte

When the holiday season rolls around, we all think of eggnog. Here is a cozy way to enjoy that seasonal favorite.

YIELD: 1 SERVING

1 shot espresso
³/₄ cup cold eggnog
2 tablespoons powdered white chocolate
2 teaspoons hazelnut syrup
Ground cinnamon
Freshly grated nutmeg

Brew the espresso and set it aside. Place the eggnog in a cold frothing pitcher and steam. Since eggnog is so rich, you will not get a lot of froth, but some will develop as you heat it through. Place the white chocolate and the hazelnut syrup in the bottom of a warm 9-ounce mug. Pour in the steamed

eggnog and stir to dissolve. Place a long-handled spoon in the mug, then cap off with the froth. Pour the shot of espresso down the center of the mug. Dust with cinnamon and nutmeg and serve immediately.

Strawberry Latte

This latte is delicious with a fresh berry scone for breakfast, or with strawberry shortcake for an early springtime dessert.

YIELD: 1 SERVING

1 shot espresso
1 teaspoon strawberry syrup
3/4 cup cold low-fat milk

Honey-Streaked Latte

This beverage is a free-form art piece in a glass—the honey streaks down the sides of the mug creating unique patterns. Be sure to serve it in a clear mug for the full effect!

YIELD: 1 SERVING

1 shot espresso
3/4 cup cold low-fat milk
2 teaspoons honey, plus several drops

Brew the espresso and set it aside. Place the milk in a cold frothing pitcher and steam. Place 2 teaspoons of the honey in the bottom of a 9-ounce mug and pour in the steamed milk.

Stir to dissolve the honey. Place a long-handled spoon in the mug, then cap off with the froth. Pour the shot of espresso down the center of the mug. Place several drops of honey around the inner edge of the mug and serve immediately.

Orgeat Cappuccino

I love cappuccino; this espresso beverage has just the right amount of espresso and steamed milk. The orgeat syrup lends a delightful almond flavor.

YIELD: 1 SERVING

1 shot espresso
1/4 cup cold low-fat milk
1 teaspoon orgeat syrup
Pinch freshly grated nutmeg

Pour the brewed espresso into a warm 5-ounce cup. Place the milk in a cold frothing pitcher and add the orgeat syrup. Steam, and then pour the steamed milk mixture into the cup. Spoon the froth on top and then dust with the nutmeg. Serve immediately.

Caramel Hazelnut Cappuccino

This is a coffee and a dessert all in one. The nutty aroma, rich coffee flavor, and caramel sweetness are heaven in a cup.

YIELD: 1 SERVING

Orgeat is an almond-flavored syrup, a preparation extracted from barley and almonds.

1 shot espresso
1 teaspoon caramel syrup
1/4 cup cold low-fat milk
1 tablespoon hazelnut syrup

Pour the brewed espresso into a warm 5-ounce cup. Stir the caramel syrup into the espresso. Place the milk in a cold frothing pitcher and add the hazelnut syrup. Steam, and then pour the milk into the cup. Spoon the froth on top and serve immediately.

Creamy Coconut Cappuccino

This is a winning combination—espresso, coconut syrup, chocolate, and frothed milk. Serve this cappuccino with coconut macaroons for a delicious dessert or afternoon treat.

YIELD: 1 SERVING

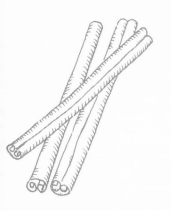

1 shot espresso
1 teaspoon coconut syrup
1/4 cup cold low-fat milk
Powdered cocoa or chocolate curls

Pour the brewed espresso into a warm 5-ounce cup. Stir in the coconut syrup. Place the milk in a cold frothing pitcher. Steam, and then pour into the cup. Spoon the froth on top and dust with powdered cocoa or add chocolate curls.

Toasted Walnut Mocha

Mocha drinks are comfort drinks. They remind us of the hot chocolate that we enjoyed before or after school. Enjoy this mocha morning or evening.

YIELD: 1 SERVING

1 shot espresso
3/4 cup cold low-fat milk
1 tablespoon unsweetened Dutch process cocoa powder
1 tablespoon walnut syrup

Brew the espresso and set it aside. Place the milk in a cold frothing pitcher and steam. Place the cocoa powder and walnut syrup in the bottom of a warm 8-ounce mug and pour in the steamed milk. Stir to dissolve the cocoa. Place a long-handled spoon in the bottom of the mug and then cap off with a bit of froth. Pour the shot of espresso down the center and serve immediately.

Raspberry Mocha

If you make this drink when fresh raspberries are in season, serve a bowl of them on the side with whipped cream. This is a great afternoon pick-me-up, and also a delicious way to start a spring day.

YIELD: 1 SERVING

1 shot espresso
¾ cup cold low-fat milk
1 tablespoon unsweetened Dutch process cocoa powder
1 tablespoon raspberry syrup

Brew the espresso and set it aside. Place the milk in a cold froth-ing pitcher and steam. Place the cocoa powder and the rasp-berry syrup in the bottom of a warm 8-ounce mug and pour in the steamed milk. Stir to dissolve the cocoa. Place a long-handled spoon in the mug and then cap off with a bit of froth. Pour the shot of espresso down the center. Serve immediately.

Sweet Mexican Mocha

This beverage is a wonderful way to begin the day. You may find your-self actually looking forward to the alarm clock's ring.

YIELD: 1 SERVING

1 shot espresso
¾ cup cold low-fat milk
1 tablespoon unsweetened Dutch process cocoa powder
1 tablespoon Mexican powdered chocolate
1 teaspoon honey

Brew the espresso and set it aside. Place the milk in a cold froth-ing pitcher and steam. Place the cocoa powder and chocolate in the bottom of a warm 8-ounce mug and pour in the steamed milk. Add the honey and stir to dissolve. Place a long-handled spoon in the mug and then cap off with the froth. Pour the shot of espresso down the center and serve immediately.

Coconut Café Mocha

This mocha reminds me of German chocolate cake! Bake your favorite recipe, or pick one up from the local bakery to serve it as a delicious dessert with this mocha.

YIELD: 1 SERVING

1 shot espresso
3/4 cup cold low-fat milk
1 tablespoon unsweetened Dutch process cocoa powder
1 tablespoon coconut syrup

Brew the espresso and briefly set it aside. Place the milk in a cold frothing pitcher and steam. Place the cocoa powder and coconut syrup in the bottom of a warm 8-ounce mug and pour in the steamed milk. Stir to dissolve the cocoa. Place a long-handled spoon in the mug and then cap off with the froth. Pour the shot of espresso down the center and serve immediately.

Hot Chocolate Drinks

All you need for most hot chocolate drinks is a heat source, a saucepan, and a mug. Add the cocoa and milk for instant pleasure. On winter evenings or around the summer campfire, hot chocolate drinks are always a cozy treat. Most of these recipes are presented to yield two servings but are easy to cut in half or multiply, depending on your needs. You may also enjoy some of these drinks cold. Simply chill them and serve in cold mugs or glasses.

Classic Hot Cocoa

Once you taste—or retaste—the goodness of "from scratch" hot cocoa it will be hard for you to go back to the instant variety. This does take a few extra minutes, but the resulting beverage is worth the time. Top with whipped cream, if desired.

YIELD: 2 SERVINGS

2 tablespoons unsweetened Dutch process cocoa powder
2 tablespoons granulated sugar
Pinch of salt
1/4 cup hot water
1 1/2 cups cold low-fat milk

Place the cocoa powder, sugar, and salt in a saucepan and gradually whisk in the hot water. Bring to a rapid simmer over medium-high heat and cook for 2 minutes, stirring constantly. Gradually pour in the milk, whisking to incorporate, and heat through but do not boil. Remove from the heat and beat with a hand-crank mixer until slightly foamy, about a minute. Pour into warm mugs and serve immediately.

Mexican Hot Chocolate

The Mexican chocolate and honey give this hot chocolate a luscious flavor. You can find Mexican-style chocolate in specialty stores or ethnic markets.

YIELD: 2 SERVINGS

2 tablespoons powdered Mexican chocolate
2 tablespoons honey
1/4 cup hot water
1 1/2 cups cold low-fat milk

Place chocolate, honey, and hot water in a saucepan and whisk to combine. Bring to a rapid simmer over medium-high heat and cook for 2 minutes, stirring constantly. Gradually pour in the milk, whisking to incorporate, and heat through but do not boil. Remove from the heat and beat with a hand-crank mixer until slightly foamy, about a minute. Pour into warm mugs and serve immediately.

Raspberry Hot Cocoa

Chocolate and raspberry syrups combine to flavor this cozy beverage. You may substitute strawberry syrup, if you wish. This is fun to serve to the little ones before bedtime—especially if a friend is sleeping over! This is also good served chilled.

YIELD: 2 SERVINGS

2 cups cold low-fat milk
1/3 cup chocolate syrup
2 teaspoons raspberry syrup

The pedigree of honey
Does not concern the bee;
A clover, any time, to him
Is aristocracy.

—Emily Dickinson

Place the milk in a small saucepan and bring to a low simmer over medium heat. Add the chocolate syrup and the raspberry syrup and whisk to combine. Pour into warm mugs and serve immediately.

Hazelnut Hot Chocolate

This hot drink is a liquid version of a chocolate candy bar with nuts! Enjoy this drink chilled as well.

YIELD: 2 SERVINGS

2 cups cold low-fat milk
1/3 cup chocolate syrup
2 teaspoons hazelnut syrup
1/4 cup whipped cream
Chocolate curls (optional)

Place the milk in a small saucepan and bring to a low simmer over medium heat. Add the chocolate syrup and the hazelnut syrup and whisk to combine. Pour into warm mugs and top with equal amounts of whipped cream. Top with some chocolate curls, if desired, and serve immediately.

Caramel Hot Cocoa

Caramel and chocolate have long been a winning combination. This hot cocoa balances the two perfectly.

2 tablespoons unsweetened Dutch process cocoa powder,
    plus additional for garnish
2 tablespoons granulated sugar
Pinch of salt
1/4 cup hot water
2 tablespoons caramel syrup
1 1/2 cups cold low-fat milk
1/4 cup whipped cream

Place the cocoa powder, sugar, and salt in a saucepan and
gradually whisk in the hot water. Bring to a rapid simmer over
medium-high heat and cook for 2 minutes, stirring constantly. Add the caramel syrup and then gradually pour in the
milk, whisking to incorporate, and heat through but do not
boil. Remove from the heat and beat with a hand-crank mixer
until slightly foamy, about a minute. Pour into warm mugs.
Top each serving with 2 tablespoons of the whipped cream
and a sprinkle of cocoa. Serve immediately.

Orange Spice Hot Chocolate

*The orange extract gives this hot chocolate a wonderful flavor. Serve
with cranberry-orange nut bread, your favorite coffee cake, or muffins
for a wonderful breakfast treat*

YIELD: 2 SERVINGS

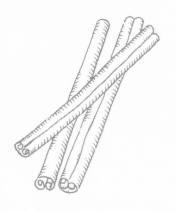

2 tablespoons unsweetened Dutch process cocoa powder
2 tablespoons granulated sugar
1/8 teaspoon ground cinnamon
Pinch of freshly ground nutmeg
Pinch of salt
1/4 teaspoon orange extract
1/4 cup hot water
1 1/2 cups cold low-fat milk
2 orange wedges (optional)

Place the cocoa, sugar, cinnamon, nutmeg, and salt in a saucepan. Gradually whisk in the orange extract and hot water. Bring to a rapid simmer over medium-high heat and cook for 2 minutes, stirring constantly. Gradually pour in the milk, whisking to incorporate, and heat through but do not boil. Remove from the heat and beat with a hand-crank mixer until slightly foamy, about a minute. Pour into warm mugs and serve immediately. Garnish each with an orange wedge, if desired.

Steamed Hot Chocolate

This is coffeehouse-style hot chocolate and is simple to make at home using your espresso machine.

YIELD: 2 SERVINGS

2 tablespoons unsweetened Dutch process cocoa powder,
     plus additional for garnish
2 teaspoons granulated sugar
2 cups cold low-fat milk
1/4 cup whipped cream

Place 1 tablespoon of the cocoa powder and 1 teaspoon of
the sugar in the bottom of each warm mug. Steam the milk
with an espresso machine according to the directions that
begin on page 105. Pour about 1/4 cup hot milk into each
mug and stir to dissolve the cocoa. Fill the mugs with the remaining milk and stir again. Top with the froth and whipped
cream. Dust with additional cocoa and serve immediately.

Milk Frothed with Chocolate and Mint

*If you like chocolate-mint ice cream, you'll love this warm version of that
delicious treat. Enjoy this frothy mug of milk as a dessert drink or as a
nightcap.*

YIELD: 2 SERVINGS

2 tablespoons chocolate syrup
2 tablespoons mint syrup
2 cups cold low-fat milk
Unsweetened Dutch process cocoa powder for garnish
     (optional)

Place 1 tablespoon each of the chocolate syrup and mint syrup in the bottom of each warm mug. Steam the milk with an espresso machine according to the directions beginning on page 105. Pour about 1/4 cup hot milk into each mug and stir to combine with the chocolate and mint syrups. Fill the mugs with the remaining milk and stir again. Top with the froth. Dust with powdered cocoa, if desired.

Walnut Vanilla Hot Chocolate

Serve this hot chocolate drink at an autumn or winter party. Gather some friends or family members, young and old, and make gingerbread houses while you sip this holiday favorite. Set out warm mugs, place the hot chocolate in a festive pitcher, and allow your guests to serve themselves.

YIELD: 8 TO 10 SERVINGS

2 quarts whole milk
8 ounces unsweetened chocolate, coarsely chopped
1 cup superfine sugar
1/4 cup toasted walnut syrup
1 tablespoon vanilla extract
2 teaspoons ground cinnamon
Several grinds fresh nutmeg

Place the milk and chocolate in a medium-size saucepan and gently heat over medium heat until the chocolate melts, about 10 minutes. Stir frequently with a wooden spoon, making sure the mixture does not come to a boil. Add the sugar, walnut syrup, vanilla, cinnamon, and nutmeg. Stir until the sugar has dissolved, 1 to 2 minutes. Pour about 1/3 of the mixture into the blender and whirl until smooth and frothy. You will have to do this in several batches so the hot liquid does not bubble over as it expands while being blended. Pour into a warm serving pitcher and serve immediately.

Vanilla Cocoa with Whipped Cream

If you are making homemade whipped cream for this recipe, add 1/2 teaspoon vanilla extract to the cream along with the sugar, and then whip until soft peaks form. This will enhance the vanilla flavor in this rich, chocolate drink. You may use prepared whipped cream with equally good results.

Yield: 8 to 10 servings

6-inch vanilla bean
3/4 cup superfine sugar
1/2 cup unsweetened Dutch process cocoa powder
Pinch of salt
3/4 cup hot water
3 cups whole milk
1 1/2 cups half-and-half
1/4 cup vanilla syrup
1 to 2 cups whipped cream

Use a sharp knife to slit the vanilla bean in half lengthwise. Set aside. Place the sugar, cocoa powder, and salt in a large saucepan. Gradually whisk in the hot water. Bring to a rapid simmer over medium heat and cook for 2 minutes, stirring constantly. Gradually pour in the milk, half-and-half, and vanilla syrup, whisking to incorporate. Increase the heat to medium-high and heat through but do not boil. Remove from the heat and discard the vanilla bean. Beat with a hand-crank mixer for several minutes, until slightly foamy. Pour into warm mugs and top with the desired amount of whipped cream. Serve immediately.

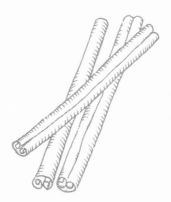

7

CLASSIC AND MODERN TOASTS

Raising the glass before encouraging guests to take a sip is a global tradition that has been passed down throughout the centuries. Recorded history tells us that ancient Greeks, as early as the sixth century B.C., are believed to have initiated the art of offering a toast. *Stin ygia sou!*—Greek for "To your health!"—was commonly offered as a general toast, then the glass would be raised by the host symbolizing to the guests that the beverage was safe to drink.

The Latin term *tostus,* "toast," originated with the Roman custom of dropping a piece of burnt bread into the wine. The charcoal would reduce the acidity of slightly off-tasting wine, thus rendering it more palatable.

The offering of a toast can be done in an informal manner by simply raising and clinking the glasses, or more formally by offering a few words—usually directed to a specific member of the group. The informal toast, directed to the guests at large, may also contain sentiments offering an expression of friendship, appreciation for the meal to come, or a global wish for health and prosperity. When glasses are clinked, a bell-like sound emanates. It is believed that this custom started as a Christian tradition to scare away the devil, who was thought to be terrified by the sound of bells. The more formal toast, however, does have some etiquette associated with it. The person to whom the toast is offered does not raise his or her glass and join in, but accepts the toast graciously and then has a sip after the others have tasted their drinks.

Offering a toast at a holiday meal is another warm tradition. Annual dinners celebrating birthdays or holidays usually call for a toast. Any member of the party may give the toast, and frequently there will be more than one toast offered. This is a great tradition to pass down from generation to generation. The senior members tend to remember toasts from previous occasions and the little ones love the whimsical formality.

A more formal dinner setting or celebratory gathering, however, usually commands that the toast be the duty of the host or hostess. You may want to memorize and practice your toast so that it rolls off your tongue without any sense of nervousness.

Offering a Toast

The following tips will put you at ease when you offer a toast.

✧ Offer the toast once all of the guests have been served a drink.

✧ Always stand when offering a toast to a large gathering.

✧ Deliver the toast from your heart.

Come fill a fresh bumper,
For why should we go,
While the nectar
   still reddens
Our cups as they flow.
Pour out the rich juices:
Still bright with the sun;
Till o'er the brimmed
   crystal
The rubies shall run.
   –Oliver Wendell Holmes

- Be eloquent, whimsical, or witty, but always make sure that the toast you are conveying is appropriate for the occasion and the group gathered.

- Keep it simple, short, and to the point.

- Be prepared by either memorizing your toast or by having key phrases written on note cards.

- Smile.

- End your toast with a common phrase such as "Cheers" or "*Salud*," then raise your glass to signify that the others should clink their glasses and take a sip.

Toasting Etiquette

If you are hosting a formal dinner in honor of a beloved person, prepare a toast in his or her honor. Set out the stemware and make sure everyone has been served, or that the bottles of wine are being passed around.

- The host or hostess should offer the first toast to a guest of honor. However, a guest may politely request the host or hostess's permission to offer a toast if it appears that no toast is intended to be offered, or to offer one following that of the host or hostess.

- Never tap on a glass to get the group's attention. It is best to stand and hold your glass high until you have the attention of most of those present.

- If the toast is being offered to you, do not stand up or take a drink until after the toast has been delivered. Then you may stand and offer a response, or simply say "thank you" and take a sip of your drink.

Favorite Toasts

Commit to memory a few of these toasts, and you will always be ready to offer one. If you are prepared, you will be at ease and comfortable addressing any gathering.

> "Here's looking at you, kid."
>
> > —Humphrey Bogart, in
> > *Casablanca*, 1942

> "May all your troubles be little ones."
>
> > —Anonymous

> "May you live all the days of your life."
>
> > —Jonathan Swift

> "God only made water, but man made wine."
>
> > —Victor Hugo

May misfortune follow you the rest of your life, but never catch up.

—Anonymous

143

May your laugh, your love,
and your wine be plenty,
thus your happiness will be
nothing less.

—Demillo

"Let us toast the fools;
But for them, the rest of us could not succeed."

—Mark Twain

"Grow old with me!
The best is yet to be,
The last of life, for which, the first is made."

—Robert Browning

"Moderation is a fatal thing—nothing succeeds
like excess."

—Oscar Wilde

"The problem with some people is that when they
aren't drunk, they're sober."

—William Butler Yeats

"May your sons be strong,
May your daughters be marriageable,
May your kinfolk be rich."

—Tennessee toast

"To the land we love and the love we land!"

—Traditional Welsh toast

"May the roof above us never fall in,
and may the friends gathered below it never fall out."

—Irish proverb

"Always remember to forget
the things that made you sad.
But never forget to remember
the things that made you glad."

—Irish proverb

"As you slide down the banister of life,
May the splinters never point the wrong way."

—Irish proverb

"Life is like a cup of tea, it's all how you make it!"

—Irish proverb

"Do not resent growing old.
Many are denied the privilege."

—Irish proverb

"May you have warm words on a cold evening,
A full moon on a dark night,
And a smooth road all the way to your door."

—Irish proverb

"The heart that loves is forever young."

—Greek proverb

"May your love be like good wine and grow stronger
as it grows older."

—English proverb

145

"Here is to health, love, and money
and the time to enjoy them!"

—Spanish proverb

"Some friends wish you happiness, and others
wish you wealth—but I wish you the best of all—
contentment blessed with health!"

—Anonymous

"May the right hand always
be stretched out in friendship and never in want."

—Irish proverb

International Toasts

Most nations also have their own traditional toast that is
comprised of only one word, or of a few short words. Here
are some that have been shared with me, or that I have heard
while traveling.

"*Rrofsh sa mallet.*" May you live as long as the hills.

—Albania

"*Salud!*" To your health!

—Argentina, Brazil,
Mexico, Spain

"*Proist!*" May it be to your health!

—Austria

"Cheers!"

—Australia, Great Britain,
United States of America

"*À votre sante and à la votre!*" To your health and
to yours!

—Canada

"*Ganbei.*" Dry your cup.

—China

"*À votre sante.*" To your health.

—France

"*Stin ygia sou!*" To your health!

—Greece

"*Skal!*" A salute to you!

—Iceland, Sweden, Norway

"*Slainthe is saol agat!*" Health and life to you!

—Ireland

"*L'chaim!*" To life!

—Israel

147

"Alla tua salute!" To your health!

—Italy

"Cin-cin!" All good things to you!

—Italy

"Kan pai!" Dry your cup!

—Japan

"Mabuhay!" Long life!

—Philippines

"Vashe zdorovie!" To health!

—Russia

"Chai yo!" To your health and well-being!

—Thailand

Acknowledgments

Gathering with friends and family to enjoy a cozy drink is such a pleasure—and writing this book provided the reason for many such gatherings. Thank you all for your encouragement and thoughtful comments. I offer a special thanks to Paul Bennett. Paul has been a friend for many years and knows his way around the back side of a bar. His knowledge of spirits, and what to pair them with, provided the foundation for many of the drink recipes. My love of coffee and cocoa drinks has spanned many years, so creating the delicious espresso, brewed coffee, and cocoa drinks was a delicious indulgence.

Jennifer Basye Sander, my editor at Prima Publishing, provided the inspiration for this book—thank you for the opportunity to work on the project. Andi Reese Brady is the best production editor a person could ask for. Andi, I appreciate your professionalism and personal touch—it comes through even in this technological age. The marketing team at Random House embraced the concept for this book with enthusiasm and creative marketing efforts.

Index